The
Home Remodeling
Management
Book

THE HOME REMODELING MANAGEMENT BOOK

*How to Plan, Organize
and Manage Your
Home Remodeling Project*

Kathryn E. Schmidt, AIA

A PERIGEE BOOK

Getting 1 **Started**

Planning 2 **Your Project**

Developing 3 **Your Budget**

Community 4 **Building Regulations**

Design 5 **Consultants**

The 6 **Design Process**

Bidding and 7 **Contractor Selection**

The 8 **Construction Process**

Furnishings 9

Perigee Books
are published by
The Putnam Publishing Group
200 Madison Avenue
New York, NY 10016

First Perigee Edition 1991

Library of Congress Cataloging-in-Publication Data

Schmidt, Kathryn.
    The home remodeling management book : how to plan, organize and
manage your home remodeling project / Kathryn Schmidt.
—1st Perigee ed.
        p.   cm.
    Reprint. Originally published: Palo Alto, Calif. : Egger
Publications, c1987.
    Includes bibliographical references (p.) and index.
    ISBN 0-399-51666-2
    1. Dwellings—Remodeling—Handbooks, manuals, etc.   2. Dwellings—
Remodeling—Forms.   I. Title.
[TH4816.S275   1991]   90-48151   CIP
643′.7—dc20

Printed in the United States of America
1   2   3   4   5   6   7   8   9   10

Acknowledgements

Thank you to all the friends who reviewed the manuscript, shared ideas and experiences and gave encouragement - Nancy Baer, Connie Cox, Marlene Grant, Kristin Meuser, Brian Peters and Lisa Stelck. A special note of gratitude to Spencer Associates, Architects and Planners and Jan Stypula for the excellent project management experience and for use of equipment and facilities. Finally, authors always thank their spouses; now I know why. Thank you most of all to my husband Sam Luoma for helpful review comments, unlimited patience and enthusiastic encouragement.

Contents

"It may be enough to realize that domestic comfort involves a range of attributes ... all of which contribute to the experience; common sense will do the rest. Most people - 'I may not know why I like it, but I know what I like' - recognize comfort when they see it."

Witold Rybczynski
Home:
A Short History of an Idea

Introduction

Each year thousands of households begin remodeling and home improvement projects ($52 billion worth in 1985 according to the National Association of the Remodeling Industry) in pursuit of more comfortable homes. But often, remodeling is <u>un</u>comfortable because many homeowners do not know what the process and their projects will include when they start out. Remodeling is complicated and it can feel "out of control" if one does not understand what is involved.

The goal of this book is to help homeowners understand and maintain control of their home remodeling projects. It explains the steps required to take a remodeling from an idea to a finished product. This book is a homeowner's detailed project management guide, planning aid and system for collecting information; it does not explain how to design or how to build. It is based on techniques that professional project managers and architects use to manage the planning, design and building process. This book will be a resource throughout any remodeling project. It outlines the details that you need to know and will help you remember to do what is necessary to obtain a good product in an organized manner. Hopefully it will bring not only organization, but also an element of comfort, to a complex process.

Each remodeling is unique, but each project requires the same careful organization and management. Whether you have a large or small project, whether you hire several professionals or only a single contractor; whether you do some construction yourself or not, you will go through the same process.

Remodeling is a challenging endeavor. It is never completely easy and carefree and the often heard statement "remodeling takes twice as much time and costs twice as much money as you first imagined" has some basis. But the rewards are very great. You solve a problem; you make your home more livable and comfortable; you help create your own living environment; you make a good investment. Then you have the pleasure of enjoying and living in the product of your successful efforts.

The
Home Remodeling
Management
Book

1

ACTION.

✔ **How to Use This Book.** 3
  ✔ Skim the short Summaries at the beginning of each chapter
    that outline the *Action* items, *Worksheets* and *Potential*
    Problems and Pitfalls of each step. 3
  ✔ Read the chapters as you need more information. 4
✔ **Set Up a Management System.** 4
  ✔ Review the *Remodeling Process* diagram. 5
  ✔ Select a Project Manager to oversee: 5
    - Achieving the design goals.
    - Staying within the budget.
    - Meeting the schedule.
  ✔ Start a system to keep track of information. 6
    - Use this book.
    - Set up a notebook or additional files.

WORKSHEETS.

✎ *The Remodeling Process* 7
✎ *The Remodeling Process* (Blank) 9
✎ *Project Directory* 11

POTENTIAL PROBLEMS AND PITFALLS.

☛Set up a management system. If you are not organized from the beginning,
your project is likely to be more difficult throughout.
☛Someone must accept the responsibility of being project manager. If not,
the result will be a disorganized project.

Getting Started

Remodeling or building an addition to your home is one of the biggest investments that you as a homeowner will ever make. But since it is a process that most of us undertake only once or twice in our lifetimes, we often begin our home remodeling projects with an incomplete picture of what we are getting into and where we are going. Every year thousands of homeowners learn from experience that remodeling involves more than collecting ideas from magazines, hiring a contractor and adding to the mortgage. It includes planning, budgets and accounting, contracts, design decisions, details, schedules, managing people and surviving the mess. It also requires hard work, persistence, patience and flexibility. Overall, managing a remodeling project is like running a small business.

This book will make home remodeling easier for those who do not make a career out of remodeling projects. It will remove some of the guesswork and help homeowners avoid the problems and pitfalls, too. This book presents an overview and an explanation of all the steps involved in planning and implementing a project from beginning to end. It also outlines the details that every homeowner should know to organize and manage a successful home remodeling project.

There are worksheets and checklists for planning, budgeting, investigating building regulations, selecting architects and contractors, making design decisions, following the construction process, keeping expense records and selecting furnishings, too. Use this book throughout your project to stay organized, to keep things under control and to remember the details that can make the difference between a good project and an "I-wish-I-had-known-that-when-I-started" project.

How to Use This Book

Each chapter of *The Home Remodeling Management Book* describes a separate step of the remodeling process and contains management forms or worksheets to use during that step. When you first start to plan your project, skim the summary page at the beginning of each chapter to get an overview of the remodeling process. The summary pages outline the *Action* items, the *Worksheets* and the *Potential Problems and Pitfalls* of each step. They also indicate page number references when you are ready for more detailed explanations in the chapters.

This book describes the steps for both renovation work and additions. Depending on the size and scope of your project, some of the details and discussion may not apply and you may need only a few of the forms to manage your remodeling. Do not be intimidated by the quantity of information and worksheets. Use the book in a way that works for you. Gather information, ask questions and fill out some of the forms or simply use the checklists to keep your project organized. Some people write everything down, some use outlines and others keep all the details in their heads.

Although the remodeling process is represented as consecutive steps, some steps may overlap (see the *Remodeling Process Diagram* in this chapter). You will also use more than one part of the book at a time to collect information. For example, you may be able to record a variety of resources and research at the beginning of your project: friends may have recommended good designers (Chapter 5) and contractors (Chapter 7); you may have thought carefully about your budget (Chapter 3); and you may have collected specifications about appliances (Chapter 6) and furniture (Chapter 9). Write that information down under the appropriate steps, add to it as you go and it will not get lost.

The *Glossary* at the end of this book contains definitions of building terms which will help you communicate with designers and contractors. The *Resources* section lists additional sources of information if you want to learn more details about specific parts of remodeling, for example, construction or interior design.

Set Up a Management System

There are three important things to do when you begin your home remodeling project:

- Get a clear picture of the steps involved in the remodeling process.
- Select someone to be responsible for managing the project from beginning to end.
- Create a system for keeping track and organizing information.

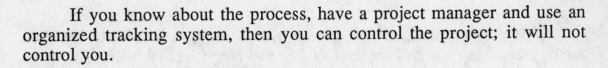

If you know about the process, have a project manager and use an organized tracking system, then you can control the project; it will not control you.

The Remodeling Process

The first diagram in this chapter illustrates *The Remodeling Process* from start to finish. The nine major steps are:

1. Getting Started
2. Planning Your Project
3. Developing Your Budget
4. Community Building Regulations
5. Design Consultants
6. The Design Process
7. Bidding and Contractor Selection
8. The Construction Process
9. Furnishings

The steps are listed on the left and are subdivided into specific events as you read across the page. Use the diagram to get an overall image of the process and to see where steps are consecutive and where they may overlap. This diagram also shows how much time it would take to complete an average remodeling project (remodel a kitchen and add a bedroom and bathroom). Each vertical division represents one month. This project took nine months to plan and build. A blank *Remodeling Process* diagram is provided for you to use to follow the progress of your own project or to make a rough estimate of how much time your project will take.

REMEMBER TO USE THIS BOOK IN A WAY THAT WORKS FOR YOU.

Project Manager

One family member should manage the project on a day to day basis. It takes someone with a keen interest in seeing the job completed, someone who is willing to spend time and energy on the project, someone who will pay attention to detail and someone who will be responsible. The project manager's primary concerns throughout the project will be:

• Achieving the design goals. (See Chapter 2)
• Staying within the budget. (See Chapter 3)
• Meeting the schedule.

The project manager need not do everything him or herself, but that person must keep track of the project and make certain that everything gets done. He or she can delegate many tasks. If a professional interior designer is employed, for example, that person will be paid to be responsible for furniture selection. If a general contractor or subcontractors are hired, they will be responsible for construction. If another family member is assigned the task of moving furniture out of the rooms to be remodeled, that will be his or her job. But the project manager must manage the process, make certain that each person understands his tasks (and the associated goals, budget and schedule) and ensure that all the necessary "Steps of Remodeling" are completed.

Keeping Track

The project manager must keep track of information and have it readily accessible throughout the remodeling process. This greatly simplifies the job. He or she will need to refer to checklists, contracts, notes and product literature and verify price quotations, decisions and dates.

Use this book as your tracking system. It is best to write things down and keep them all in one place. In addition to the worksheets, there is plenty of space to take notes. Supplement this book with a three ring binder or files where you can keep design ideas, photographs, articles, contracts, invoices, correspondence and any other pertinent information. You may even want to take the book apart and put it in your binder so you can maintain all your records in a single book.

The telephone is another important element in keeping track. The project manager will need to manage people, check on their progress, arrange meetings and communicate decisions. There may be only one or two people involved or there may be several (examples are the lender, the architect, the interior designer and/or the contractor). Use the *Project Directory* in this chapter to record their names, addresses and phone numbers.

NOW, SHARPEN YOUR PENCIL AND GET STARTED! ■

The Remodeling Process

Getting 1 Started
Using this book and getting organized.

- How to use this book.
- Take an organized approach.
  - Review this diagram.
  - Select a project manager.
  - Set up a tracking system.

Planning 2 Your Project
Examining what you have and formulating a Master Plan.

- Examine what you have now.
- Formulate a Master Plan.
  - Establish your long term goals.
  - Analyze what you want to change.
  - Set your priorities.

Developing 3 Your Budget
Establishing an investment target and estimating how much the project will cost.

- Establish an Investment Target.
- Estimate Project Costs.
- Balance the budget equation.

Community 4 Building Regulations
Reviewing community regulations and visiting the building department.

- Visit your community offices to learn what zoning, planning and building regulations require and allow.
- Obtain building permit.

Design 5 Consultants
Deciding if you want a design consultant; then finding and hiring one.

- Find and interview designers.
- Select a designer.
- Sign a contract with the designer.

The 6 Design Process
Taking your remodeling project from ideas to completed drawings.

- Predesign.
- Preliminary Design.
- Final Design.

Bidding and 7 Contractor Selection
Finding contractors and obtaining a price for construction.

- Find and interview contractors.
- Obtain bids for construction.
- Select a contractor.
- Sign a contract with the contractor.

The 8 Construction Process
What happens and what you should do before, during and after construction.

- Before construction begins.
  - Paperwork.
  - Preconstruction meeting.
  - Family plans.
- Preparation and rough construction.
- Closing in the new work
- Finishing the work.
- Closing out the project.

Furnishings 9
Selecting and purchasing furnishings.

- Shop for furnishings.
- Order furnishings
- Furnishings arrive.

Month 1	Month 2	Month 3	Month 4	Month 5	Month 6	Month 7	Month 8	Month 9

The Remodeling Process

	Month 1	Month 2	Month 3	Month 4	Month 5	Month 6	Month 7	Month 8	Month 9
Getting 1 Started — Using this book and getting organized.									
Planning 2 Your Project — Examining what you have and formulating a Master Plan.									
Developing 3 Your Budget — Establishing an investment target and estimating how much the project will cost.									
Community 4 Building Regulations — Reviewing community regulations and visiting the building department.									
Design 5 Consultants — Deciding if you want a design consultant; then finding and hiring one.									
The 6 Design Process — Taking your remodeling project from ideas to completed drawings.									
Bidding and 7 Contractor Selection — Finding contractors and obtaining a price for construction.									
The 8 Construction Process — What happens and what you should do before, during and after construction.									
Furnishings 9 — Selecting and purchasing furnishings.									

Notes

Project Directory

Owner ————————————————

Address ————————————————

————————————————

Phone ————————————————

Contact ————————————————

Architect ————————————————

Address ————————————————

————————————————

Phone ————————————————

Contact ————————————————

Interior Designer ————————————

Address ————————————————

————————————————

Phone ————————————————

Contact ————————————————

Landscape Arch. ——————————

Address ————————————————

————————————————

Phone ————————————————

Contact ————————————————

Structural Engineer ————————

Address ————————————————

————————————————

Phone ————————————————

Contact ————————————————

Other ————————————————

Address ————————————————

————————————————

Phone ————————————————

Contact ————————————————

Financial Inst. ——————————

Address ————————————————

————————————————

Phone ————————————————

Contact ————————————————

Building Dept. ——————————

Address ————————————————

————————————————

Phone ————————————————

Contact ————————————————

Other ————————————————

Address ————————————————

————————————————

Phone ————————————————

Contact ————————————————

Other ————————————————

Address ————————————————

————————————————

Phone ————————————————

Contact ————————————————

Other ————————————————

Address ————————————————

————————————————

Phone ————————————————

Contact ————————————————

Other ————————————————

Address ————————————————

————————————————

Phone ————————————————

Contact ————————————————

General Contractor —————————

Address —————————

—————————

Phone —————————
Contact —————————

Other —————————

Address —————————

—————————

Phone —————————
Contact —————————

Other —————————

Address —————————

—————————

Phone —————————
Contact —————————

Other —————————

Address —————————

—————————

Phone —————————
Contact —————————

Furniture Store —————————

Address —————————

—————————

Phone —————————
Contact —————————

Other —————————

Address —————————

—————————

Phone —————————
Contact —————————

Other Contractor —————————

Address —————————

—————————

Phone —————————
Contact —————————

Other —————————

Address —————————

—————————

Phone —————————
Contact —————————

Other —————————

Address —————————

—————————

Phone —————————
Contact —————————

Other —————————

Address —————————

—————————

Phone —————————
Contact —————————

Furniture Store —————————

Address —————————

—————————

Phone —————————
Contact —————————

Other —————————

Address —————————

—————————

Phone —————————
Contact —————————

Notes

2

ACTION.

WORKSHEETS.

POTENTIAL PROBLEMS AND PITFALLS.

☛Formulate a Master Plan for your home. Your remodeling will be more effective. It is much better to have a plan that you change than to have no plan at all.

☛It is very likely that you will change your mind about both major and minor parts of your home remodeling as the project progresses. This is normal and it is generally not a problem if you make changes during design. Just remember that as you go further into the process, it will become more difficult to make significant changes. (It may cost more money and take more time.)

☛Make certain that family decision makers agree to the project and to the priorities. It will prevent unnecessary conflict.

Planning Your Project

Planning is determining the current needs and long-term goals for your home. The design of actual floor plans comes later. Thoughtful planning at the beginning of your project will help you organize and implement your remodeling ideas.

Most likely you can list thirty problems in your kitchen that need immediate attention, and you would start construction tomorrow if possible. Before you rush to solve the most prominent problem, take some time to think about your entire house. Assess what you have now. Then think about what you want in the future, determine what you want to change and set priorities. In other words, formulate a Master Plan for your home. If you look at your entire home and your long-term goals first, your plans for specific areas will be more effective and you may be able to solve several problems at once. You can modify the Master Plan if your needs change over time.

Planning also includes formulating a budget and finding out what your community building regulations will allow. Although budgeting and building regulations are discussed separately in Chapters 3 and 4, it is useful to do some work on each in conjunction with the planning in this chapter because all are related. For example, familiarizing yourself with the *Estimated Project Cost* section of Chapter 3 will help you to be more realistic about remodeling plans and priorities. Or if you want to convert the garage to a family room, Chapter 4 describes how to find out if your community will require that you build a new garage or carport to replace the old garage.

Use the worksheets in this chapter (they are explained on the following pages) to develop a Master Plan. This written plan will be the basis of the design solutions for your current and future remodeling projects.

Examine What You Have Now

Survey your home thoroughly and record information about the existing conditions.

Outline a Description of Your Home

First, outline the basic facts about your home (size of house and lot, deed restrictions, materials) on the *Existing Home Description* worksheet which follows the discussion in this chapter. This is routine information, but much of it will be requested during the course of your project by lenders, the building department and others. You may have to consult your deed or other purchase documents to find the assessor's parcel number and deed restrictions.

Assess its Condition

Next, look at your home very closely to assess its condition inside and out. Look at the lot and walk completely around the house. Observe its relationship to the neighbors. Go through every room. Take photographs of the interior and exterior so you can examine it more objectively. What are your home's good points and bad points? Look for areas that may need repairs and maintenance. (If you are unsure about assessing the physical condition of your home, you can hire a professional building inspection service to do it. Look in the Yellow Pages of your telephone directory. Check references for any inspection service you plan to hire just as you would with any professional.) Write your notes on the *Home Assessment* worksheet which follows the *Home Description*. Attach photographs on the next page. They will be a handy reference when you need to remember details about the house. (They will look great in "before and after" comparisons, too.)

Diagram the Floor Plan

It is also useful to diagram the floor plan of your home. This will help you visualize how your home functions now and make plans for future changes. Use the *Existing Floor Plan* worksheet following the photograph page to make a plan diagram. Measure the rooms and show specific dimensions or simply make a bubble diagram to illustrate room relationships. If you want to make more detailed drawings of your home, there are many books available to help you (see the *Resources* section.) If drawing plan diagrams is not your forte, you can hire a professional to do all necessary drawings during the design phase. If you have existing drawings of your home, this task is already completed.

If you plan to add new rooms, it is important to know where your house is located in relationship to your property lines and the required building setbacks. Your property dimensions will be described in your deed. Measure the distance from the house to the edge of the property in all critical directions. If you have existing drawings, the house location will probably be indicated. If not, your community Building Department may have records showing its location. In a rare circumstance it may be difficult to locate your house in relationship to property lines and setbacks. You may need to hire a civil engineer to help.

Formulate a Master Plan

Think about what you want in the future and record your priorities for change.

Establish Long-Term Goals

After examining your home, think about long-range goals. Do you plan to stay in this home for several years or are you going to sell it soon? Will the number of family members at home grow or shrink in the near future? How do you want your home to look and function? List your goals on the *Home Goals* worksheet. This exercise will help you set the context for remodeling. If your goals are to make home improvements for selling the house in a few years, you probably will want to spend less time, effort and money than if you plan to stay a long time. If you plan to live in your home for several years, you may want to divide your remodeling goals into separate projects for gradual implementation.

Analyze What You Want to Change

Next, study your home "problem" areas. Examine each room that you want to change or add. How are the rooms used? What furnishings and appliances are located in each room? What do you like about the rooms and what changes would you like to make? This information will help during the design process. Use the *Room Analysis and Planning* worksheets; complete one for each room that you want to change. If you would like, diagram proposed changes on the *Floor Plan Changes* worksheet provided.

Set Your Priorities

Then review your home analysis and make a list of proposed changes including maintenance and repair projects. After consulting the family decision makers, prioritize the changes on the *Changes and Priorities* worksheet. This worksheet will be your Master Plan. It will help you decide which areas are most important and where you want to spend money first if you do not make all the changes at once.

WHEN YOU SET PRIORITIES FOR CHANGE, IT IS VERY IMPORTANT THAT THE FAMILY DECISION MAKERS AGREE. Remodeling is a stressful experience. It can emphasize personal differences and shake good relationships. If you see conflicts at the beginning, it is much easier to resolve them early than to wait until walls have been removed. It may be perfectly acceptable that this is "his" project or "her" project, but agree in the planning stage so everyone can work happily toward the same goals.   ▪

Existing Home Description

OWNER _____ Date _____

Address _____

_____ Phone No. _____

LOT INFORMATION:

Lot Size (Dimensions) _____ Area of Lot (Sq Ft) _____

Assessor's Parcel Number _____ Flat or Sloping _____

Deed Restrictions _____

_____

_____

Landscaping _____

HOUSE INFORMATION:

House Built In (Year) _____ Front Faces Toward:

North ____ East ____ South ____ West ____

Number of Stories _____ Area of House (Sq Ft) _____

Number of Rooms:

Living Rm ____	Bedrooms ____	Family Rm ____	Garage ____ cars
Dining Rm ____	Bathrooms ____	Study/Office ____	Carport ____ cars
Kitchen ____	Other ____		

Amenities:

Fireplace ____	Decks ____	Patios ____	Greenhouse ____
Swim Pool ____	Tennis Ct ____	Other ____	Other ____

Materials:

Exterior Walls _____	Roof _____
Interior Walls _____	Floors _____
Ceilings _____	Cabinets _____
Doors _____	Windows _____
Type of Heating _____	Air Conditioning _____

Other: _____

_____

_____

_____

Home Assessment

What are the assets and liabilities of the lot?

- Landscaping: Preserve ———————   Change ———————
- Views: Within Lot ——————— Away from Lot ———————

———————————————   ———————————————

- Other Structures: Good ———————   Need Repair ———————
  (Garage, fence, shed) ———————————————
- Environmental Factors: No Problem ——————— Need work ———————
  (Sun, wind, noise and traffic) ———————————————

———————————————————————————————

What is the condition of the house?

Exterior
- Foundation or basement: ———————————————————
- Exterior walls: ———————————————————
- Roof and gutters: ———————————————————
- Patios, decks, porches: ———————————————————
- Other ———————————————————

———————————————————————————————

Interior
- Living Spaces: ———————————————————
- Kitchen: ———————————————————
- Bathrooms: ———————————————————
- Bedrooms: ———————————————————
- Electrical, heating, air conditioning: ———————————
- Other ———————————————————

———————————————————————————————

Are any major repairs or maintenance needed?

(Examples: new roof, repair water damage, new paint.)

- ———————————————   - ———————————————
- ———————————————   - ———————————————
- ———————————————   - ———————————————

What are the good points and bad points about the house?

(Examples: sunny rooms, good views .... small kitchen, dark living room.)

- ———————————————   - ———————————————
- ———————————————   - ———————————————
- ———————————————   - ———————————————

Photographs of Existing Home

Date_____

Use this page to attach photographs of your existing home BEFORE your home remodeling.

Photographs of Existing Home

Date _____

Use this page to attach photographs of your existing home BEFORE your home remodeling.

Existing Floor Plan

Use this page to diagram your existing floor plan or the basic relationships among rooms.

Each square on this grid is 1/4"x1/4"

Existing Floor Plan

Use this page to diagram your existing floor plan or the basic relationships among rooms.

Each square on this grid is 1/4"x1/4"

Home Goals

The primary goal of remodeling this home is:
- To create a more comfortable living environment. _____
- To get a better return on investment when the house is sold._____

We / I plan to live in this home for the next _____ years.   During these years:
- Family use will stay the same. _____
- There will be more/fewer children. _____ How many? _____ When? _____
- There will be more/fewer adults.   _____ How many? _____ When? _____
- A family member will work out of a home office. _____
- We would like to have a room/unit to rent. _____
- Other _____
  _____
  _____
  _____

Describe how you would like your home to function to suit your style of living.
(Examples: more private spaces, bigger rooms, better access to outdoor patios and decks,
more open floor plan, easier maintenance, more space for entertaining, music in every room,
more natural light, better rooms for kids, better space for sports fans.)

_____
_____
_____
_____
_____
_____

How do you envision your home?
(Examples: formal, informal, private retreat, separate areas for children and adults,
an active place with projects happening everywhere, everything clean and put away,
place for entertaining.)

_____
_____
_____
_____

Room Analysis and Planning

ROOM ——————————————— **Size** ———————————————

Use a separate form for each room you want to change. Think about whether space is used efficiently and if paint/wallpaper/carpet, rearranging and/or repairs will solve your problems.

How is the room used?

What functions happen in the room? ———————————————
———————————————————————————————

Who uses the room? ———————————————
When and how often is it used? ———————————————
What rooms/functions should be nearby? ———————————————
———————————————————————————————

What things are in the room?

What furnishings and appliances are there? ———————————————
———————————————————————————————

What do you store in the room (and its shelves and closets)? ———————————————
———————————————————————————————

What do you like about the room?
———————————————
———————————————
———————————————

Diagram the existing room here.

What would you like to change?

Size ———————————————
Function ———————————————
Furnishings/Appliances
———————————————
Doors/Windows ———————————————
Storage ———————————————
Lighting ———————————————
Other ———————————————

What mental images do you have for this room? (Examples: cozy, light, formal, comfortable, old fashioned)

———————————————
———————————————
———————————————

Each square is 1/4"x1/4"

Room Analysis and Planning

ROOM ———————————————— **Size** ————————————————————

Use a separate form for each room you want to change. Think about whether space is used efficiently and if paint/wallpaper/carpet, rearranging and/or repairs will solve your problems.

How is the room used?
What functions happen in the room? ————————————————————

——

Who uses the room? ————————————————————————
When and how often is it used? ————————————————————
What rooms/functions should be nearby? ———————————————

——

What things are in the room?
What furnishings and appliances are there? ——————————————

——

What do you store in the room (and its shelves and closets)? ———————

——

What do you like about the room?

————————————————————
————————————————————
————————————————————

What would you like to change?
Size ——————————————
Function ——————————————
Furnishings/Appliances

————————————————————
Doors/Windows ——————————
Storage ——————————————
Lighting ——————————————
Other ——————————————

What mental images do you have for this room? (Examples: cozy, light, formal, comfortable, old fashioned)

————————————————————
————————————————————
————————————————————

Diagram the existing room here.

Each square is 1/4"x1/4"

Room Analysis and Planning

ROOM _____ **Size** _____

Use a separate form for each room you want to change. Think about whether space is used efficiently and if paint/wallpaper/carpet, rearranging and/or repairs will solve your problems.

How is the room used?

What functions happen in the room? _____

_____

Who uses the room? _____

When and how often is it used? _____

What rooms/functions should be nearby? _____

_____

What things are in the room?

What furnishings and appliances are there? _____

_____

What do you store in the room (and its shelves and closets)? _____

_____

What do you like about the room?

_____

_____

_____

Diagram the existing room here.

What would you like to change?

Size _____

Function _____

Furnishings/Appliances

_____

Doors/Windows _____

Storage _____

Lighting _____

Other _____

What mental images do you have for this room? (Examples: cozy, light, formal, comfortable, old fashioned)

_____

_____

_____

Each square is 1/4"x1/4"

Floor Plan Changes

Use this page to diagram the changes you would like to make to your home.

Each square on this grid is 1/4"x1/4"

Floor Plan Changes

Use this page to diagram the changes you would like to make to your home.

Each square on this grid is 1/4"x1/4"

Changes and Priorities
(Master Plan)

List the changes you want to make including maintenance and repair projects; then prioritize them.

CHANGES

- _____
- _____
- _____
- _____
- _____
- _____
- _____
- _____
- _____
- _____
- _____
- _____

PRIORITIES

1 _____
2 _____
3 _____
4 _____
5 _____
6 _____
7 _____
8 _____
9 _____
10 _____
11 _____
12 _____

AGREEMENT

We agree to the changes and priorities listed above.

_____   _____

Date _____   Date _____

3

ACTION.

WORKSHEETS.

POTENTIAL PROBLEMS AND PITFALLS.

☛BE SURE TO DEVELOP A BUDGET PLAN! Inadequate budget planning will allow project costs to get out of control. This is one of the major pitfalls of home remodeling. Review all the elements that contribute to cost and try to be realistic about how much your TOTAL project costs will be. It is easy to underestimate. Plan an allowance that includes room to make additions and changes.

☛If you try to save money by acting as your own general contractor or by doing a major part of the work yourself, a pitfall is underestimating how much TIME, EFFORT, COORDINATION and KNOWLEDGE is required. Investigate thoroughly before you make this decision.

Developing Your Budget

After you analyze your home and prioritize changes, the next step in remodeling is developing a budget. Your budget will help determine the size and scope of the project. IT IS IMPORTANT THAT YOU PLAN YOUR BUDGET AT THE BEGINNING OF YOUR PROJECT. If you develop a budget at this stage, you are unlikely to waste time, effort and money pursuing a home remodeling project that will cost more than you want to spend.

There are two basic parts to the budget equation:

1. **The Investment Target**
(How much money do you want to invest in this project?)

2. **The Project Costs**
(How much will this project cost?)

This is somewhat like the "chicken and the egg" problem. When you contact professionals (contractors, designers, lenders) with questions about remodeling costs, they will usually ask how much you want to spend. Your reaction most likely will be that you can not decide how much to spend until you know how much different alternatives will cost. A good way to approach this budget problem is to consider both the investment and cost sides of the equation and work on both until they are approximately equal. Although making exact budget calculations is difficult (if not impossible) at this stage, making an estimate will help determine if your remodeling is economically feasible.

Read the discussion in this chapter and then use the worksheets that follow to make your estimate. You may want to contact local sources for current cost information to refine the estimate. Return to this section any time to revise and update. If your estimated cost is more than you want to invest, this chapter includes a list of *Ways to Save Money*.

The Investment Target

Estimating how much you want to invest in home remodeling involves evaluating the following factors. Use the *Investment Target* worksheet in this chapter when you examine those factors.

How the Value of Your Home <u>After Remodeling</u> Will Fit Into Your Neighborhood

Ask one or more real estate agents to appraise the current market value of your home as it exists. Then determine the selling prices for homes recently sold in your neighborhood. Examine prices both of homes comparable to yours (those of similar size, number of rooms, age and condition) and of the best homes (those comparable in size and quality to what yours will be after it is remodeled). A real estate agent may be willing to help or tell you where to find the prices.

The <u>best</u> comparable homes in your neighborhood help define recommended limits for the maximum expected market value of your home. The National Association of Home Builders suggests that the current market value of your home plus the cost of remodeling, should not be more than 20% greater than the top comparable homes. However, if you plan to stay in this home for many years, neighborhood values are much less important. The comfort of your family may be worth the extra expense. Another consideration is how long you have lived in your home. If you have lived there for a long time, the original cost may be far below current market value. In this case, even a significant investment in remodeling may keep your total investment within neighborhood values. Again, a real estate agent who is familiar with your neighborhood should be able to give you good advice about your investment.

Your Estimates for Investment Recovery

It is difficult to predict exactly how much a remodeling project will add to the selling value of your home. It is rarely a one-to-one relationship where each dollar spent on remodeling increases the selling value by a like amount. Also tastes change, although more gradually in homes than in fashion, so that what was popular in homes last year may be less desirable this year.

A remodeled kitchen usually adds the most to a home's value and you can expect to recover much of the cost if you sell your home a year later. Adding a third bedroom to a two bedroom home or adding a second bathroom to a one bathroom home tends to increase the value, but additional bedrooms and bathrooms beyond those will not contribute as much to the value. Maintenance and repairs (for example, a new roof or foundation improvements) will add little if anything to the value. However, a few thousand dollars worth of cosmetic repairs usually makes a home easier to sell and increases the selling price by at least the amount of the investment. See the *Rules of Thumb for Estimating Investment Recovery* below.

■ RULES OF THUMB FOR ESTIMATING INVESTMENT RECOVERY ■

If you sell your home one year after improvements are completed, estimate that you will recover a portion of your additional investment as listed below.

Item	Estimated Recovery (Percent of construction cost)		
New Construction (Additional room)	40%	to	75%
Remodeled Kitchen	75%	to	125%
Remodeled Bathroom	50%	to	100%
New Garage	60%	to	100%
New Wood Deck	50%	to	60%
New Fireplace	50%	to	100%
New Landscaping	20%	to	50%
Replace Windows and Doors	30%	to	40%

Sources: Chicago Federal Savings and Loan Association, *Popular Mechanics*, and *U.S. News and World Report* all as cited in the *San Francisco Examiner and Chronicle. Real Estate Today.*

How You Finance the Project

There are three basic sources of funds for a remodeling project:

- Using savings
- Converting investments to cash
- Borrowing money

Many people use a combination of sources, but most borrow a significant portion of the required amount. See the discussion of *Types of*

Loans for a list of alternatives for borrowing. If all sources are available, select the best overall investment opportunity. It may be appropriate to consult an investment advisor to help analyze your alternatives.

How Much You Are Willing to Spend

Even if your neighborhood will support a large additional investment in your home and you can obtain the necessary money easily, you must consider how much you feel comfortable investing. There are psychological limits as well as income limits which determine how much you are willing to spend. You must decide what is appropriate.

TYPES OF LOANS

There are several types of loans available for home remodeling. Although the terminology varies, the primary categories of loans are listed below. When you research loan alternatives, be sure to collect the same information from each lender and determine what requirements each has for a loan application. You can use the *Financing Checklist* in this chapter as a basis for asking questions when you interview prospective lenders.

- **Loans based on your home equity as collateral.**
  The equity in your home is the difference between its market value and the amount you owe on the mortgage. Home equity loan rates are usually higher than regular mortgage loans and repayment periods are shorter - 5 to 15 years. Home equity loans include:
    - Second mortgage
    - Home improvement loan
    - Home equity loan
    - Federal Housing Administration (FHA) loan (Limited funding available)

- **Refinancing your mortgage.**
  Refinancing is most often used if the following criteria apply: current lending rates are lower than your existing loan rate by two percentage points, you plan to spend more than $20,000 and you plan to stay in your home another three to five years. In effect it packages your loans so you can make a single payment. You also must have enough equity in your home to pay for the remodeling. Usually a lender will loan up to 80% of the current market value of your home. The new loan pays off the original mortgage and you have the remaining money for your project.

TYPES OF LOANS

- **Unsecured personal loans.**
  Personal loans are based solely on your ability to pay (there is no collateral) and they are guaranteed by your signature.
    - Line of credit loan
      (Best if you need $5,000 or less. Usually carries higher interest rate but no closing costs.)
    - Private party loan
      (Borrowing from relatives or friends. It is wise to draw up loan documents, have an appropriate interest rate and make regular payments.)

- **Borrowing against insurance.**
  If you have built up a cash value in a life insurance policy, you can usually borrow against it as described in your policy document. Be aware that if something happens to the insured before the loan is repaid, the policy's proceeds will be reduced by the amount owed.

- **Borrowing against investments.**
  You can also use the market value of stocks and bonds as collateral for borrowing. However, if the market value of these securities falls significantly, you may be asked to repay part of the loan immediately.

- **Borrowing from corporate savings plans.**
  Many companies have savings and profit sharing plans which allow vested employees to borrow against plan amounts held in their names. Payroll deductions are often the method of repayment. If you leave the company before the loan is paid off, the amount owed will be deducted from the total which you receive from your plan.

The Estimated Project Costs

Homes are built with relatively "low-tech" processes compared to most high cost products that we buy. Imagine the problems of estimating the cost of a new car (let alone managing its construction) if that car were designed just for you, the car had to be assembled in your garage and the car builder hired different workmen to build each car that he sold.

The estimate of remodeling costs that you make during the budget development stage will be very general. Until you have detailed construction plans, it is difficult to list all the necessary parts and determine exactly how much they will cost. However, a rough estimate is very important in helping you decide the scope of your project and in keeping track of the budget target.

The total cost of your remodeling project comprises not only the direct construction cost but also related costs such as consultant fees, costs of permits and reviews, financing costs, cost of furnishings and miscellaneous costs (a catch-all category.) These costs are often unexpected and may be the difference between an affordable project and one that stretches your spending limits far beyond what you anticipated. If you plan allowances for "other costs", you are much less likely to be surprised. The other costs are described in more detail below and in associated chapters. Be sure to consider them in your budget plan.

Another word about costs - COSTS VARY. The cost of building materials and labor varies widely throughout the country just as the cost of living varies. They also change from year to year and month to month: costs will rise if there is a shortage or a strike and decline if materials and labor are abundant. The unfortunate fact is that costs are a moving target, but it is far better to have a general target than none at all.

The following paragraphs describe categories which make up the total project cost. Use the worksheets and the rules of thumb in this chapter to develop your *Estimated Project Costs*. (This discussion assumes that a homeowner does none of the work him or herself; he or she hires a designer to prepare plans and a general contractor to build the project.)

Cost of Construction

The cost of construction is the cost of labor and materials required to build a project. If a general contractor builds your project, it is the amount of his bid (or the negotiated price) and includes the contractor's overhead and profit.

In the preliminary stages, estimates are often made on a "per square foot" basis. If your project is very simple, new construction will probably cost 50% to 75% more than remodeling existing rooms. But if you are making major changes or planning to use expensive materials, remodeling costs can easily exceed new construction costs. Kitchens and bathrooms cost more to remodel than other rooms because of the concentration of plumbing, electrical work and cabinetry and they may be estimated on a "per room" basis.

Refer to the numbers listed on the *Rules of Thumb for Estimating Construction Costs* when you make your estimate. All the costs listed indicate a range of numbers. (Use the low part of the range if you live in an area where the cost of living is low; use the high part or a mid-range number as your local cost of living dictates.) You can verify local construction costs by calling contractors. Sometimes lenders or realtors can provide local cost information, too. Then calculate how much area you plan to remodel or add:

Measure the existing rooms to be remodeled and calculate the area. Or estimate the size of an addition by calculating the area of a similar space. Multiply the remodeled and/or new areas by the appropriate square foot costs (on the *Estimated Project Costs* sheet) to find your total estimated construction cost. If you prefer, use the average cost per room to make your estimate.

$

■ RULES OF THUMB FOR ESTIMATING CONSTRUCTION COSTS ■

These numbers indicate the range of construction costs throughout the United States in 1986. Use the lower numbers if you live in an area where the cost of living is low; use a middle or a high number if you live where costs are higher. Verify local building costs by contacting local sources such as contractors, lenders or realtors. If you plan to use the best (and most expensive) building materials or if you live in a <u>very</u> expensive area, increase the figures by 25% to 30%. (It is assumed that all construction work is done by a general contractor.)

Item	Cost		
New Construction (Addition)	$65 to $120 per square foot		
Remodeling (Existing space)	$40 to $100 per square foot		
Remodeled Kitchen (Major)	$25,000	to	$60,000
Remodeled Kitchen (Upgrade)	$10,000	to	$20,000
Remodeled Bathroom	$5,000	to	$20,000
New Garage	$10,000	to	$25,000
New Wood Deck	$5,000	to	$10,000
New Fireplace	$4,000	to	$8,000

Consultant Fees

You <u>may</u> require the services of one or more consultants to help with your remodeling project. Each consultant will charge professional fees for his or her work. You are most likely to hire someone to assist with design, such as an architect or interior designer, but you may need additional engineering help if you make major structural changes (add a second story or eliminate several interior walls) or if your community has special engineering requirements.

If you are considering a major project (more than $25,000), plan an allowance of 15% to 20% of estimated construction cost to cover all consultant fees for full services (design, construction drawings and contract administration) including interior design. Consultant fees will be less if you want only design ideas. Most designers will work on an hourly basis to develop design sketches. Refer to the *Rules of Thumb for Estimating Consultant Fees*. Chapter 5 explains more about design assistance and will help you refine your estimate.

RULES OF THUMB FOR ESTIMATING CONSULTANT FEES

Consultants charge a wide range of rates for their services. Rates depend on the amount of work they do, the size of the project and their experience and reputation. Consultants may also work for an agreed upon total amount (lump sum) to perform specific tasks.

Consultant	Cost
Architect	10% to 15% of constr. cost or $30 to $120 per hour
Interior Designer	50% to 100% markup on wholesale cost of furniture or $30 to $120 per hour
Landscape Architect	7% to 12% of landscape cost or $30 to $100 per hour
Engineer	1.5% to 2% of constr. cost or $30 to $100 per hour
Drafter	$20 to $40 per hour

Permits and Reviews

During the design and construction process, you probably will be required to pay fees to your local community (city or county) for granting approval of your project. The requirements vary widely from community to community, but the fees are usually relatively small. The most frequently required fee is for a building permit. However, if you live in an area with strict architectural controls, you may face architectural review or zoning approval as well. Some communities have additional permit requirements. See the next chapter on *Community Building Regulations*.

When you make your budget estimate, plan an allowance that is 1.5% to 2% of estimated construction cost for permits and reviews.

Cost of Financing

Obtaining financing for your project carries many associated costs. The largest of these costs will be points. (Points are basically a loan fee and one point equals one percent of the loan amount.) Lenders have been charging one to three points for a loan in recent years. Lenders typically charge more points when loan money is scarce and fewer points when loan money is more available. Other charges, which may include appraisal fee, title search and loan insurance, usually total a few hundred dollars. In addition, you may want to hire an attorney to help close the loan. When you research loan alternatives, be sure to ask the lender for a list of all the required fees. Use the *Financing Checklist* in this chapter to collect information.

Plan an allowance of 4% of estimated construction cost to cover the costs of financing.

Cost of Furnishings and Special Finishes

If you are remodeling existing rooms, you may be able to reuse existing furnishings or add a minimum of new pieces to complete the project. Applying new upholstery to existing furniture is a way to achieve a fresh and different look for a moderate cost. If you are making major changes or adding new rooms, plan a portion of the budget for furnishings. (Sometimes new rooms stand nearly empty for a year or two because all the money was used on construction.)

Estimating the cost of furnishings is just as difficult as estimating the cost of construction. Although rules of thumb are hard to define, a good way to obtain an rough figure is to make a list of the furnishings you might want; then call or visit a furniture store to find out their approximate costs. Catalogs or newspaper advertisements are also a source of cost information. It is not necessary to find the exact furnishings to make an estimate. Just learn approximate prices for "a sofa" or "a dining room set". Then total the costs for an estimate.

Special finishes include carpeting, wallpaper and window coverings. These items are frequently excluded from a construction contract, but usually require installation by a skilled person. Estimate the cost of special finishes the same way you estimated furnishings. Measure or calculate the size of your rooms (or windows), then visit an appropriate store or supplier to learn about costs. Be sure to ask about the cost of both materials and installation.

Miscellaneous Costs

Miscellaneous costs encompass everything else that might happen. Most miscellaneous costs will be devoted to changes which occur during construction. Changes happen for two primary reasons. First, they may be required because unexpected conditions are present inside existing floors, walls, ceilings and foundations. It is impossible for an architect or contractor to predict exactly how a home is built until the contractor begins demolition. Existing problems may require additional expenditure to correct. Second, the homeowner will inevitably want to make changes during construction (for example, add windows, cabinets, electrical outlets, and so on). Most changes can be accommodated with few problems, but they require extra work at extra cost. The chapter on *The Construction Process* explains more about changes.

Other miscellaneous costs might include moving and rental expenses if you move out of your home during construction. Planning an allowance or contingency of 15% to 25% of estimated construction cost will help provide for miscellaneous costs.

Balancing the Budget Equation

After you develop the investment and cost sides of the budget equation, compare the two. If estimated costs are 10% to 15% greater than the investment target, your budget plan will probably work because the planned allowances will provide flexibility. But if your estimated costs are much larger than your investment target, you should reexamine your plans and review the section in this chapter on *Ways to Save Money*. (Do not give up; you can still achieve something that you want.)

Your budget plan is a guide for keeping track of costs throughout the project. Some costs will be higher than estimated and some will be lower. Return to the *Estimated Project Costs* worksheet to update your figures when you have new information. Refine the estimates, make adjustments and allocate the allowance that you planned for extras as necessary. If you see a budget problem coming, you can change your plans in plenty of time to avoid a large budget overrun.

There is also an *Actual Cost* worksheet to keep track of exact costs as they occur. Unlike purchasing a car or television set, you will not know for certain how much the TOTAL project cost until it is completed. ∎

There are several ways to reduce the cost of a home remodeling project, but many will require more time and effort. Decreasing the size of the project or building it in phases can help cut costs. Doing some work yourself can save money, if you have the time and the skills. (It is assumed in the estimate that the homeowner does no construction work.)

The following list enumerates possibile ways to save money.

- **Decrease the size of the project.**
  You may be able to save money by decreasing the size of the rooms you want to add or by remodeling a smaller area. If that is undesirable, review the other possibilities.

- **Build the project in phases.**
  Build part of the project now and part of it later. Although this will not reduce the overall cost of the project (and may actually increase it with inflation and repeated start-up costs), incremental spending over a period of time may be more affordable than one large expenditure.

- **Minimize design fees.**
  If you know what plan changes you want, you may be able to work directly with a general contractor and eliminate design consultant fees.

  If you want design alternatives, hire a designer to prepare design concepts or schematic drawings only rather than complete construction drawings. Most architects and designers will work on an hourly or lump sum basis for design concepts. (You might expect to pay only 15% to 20% of the total design fees for design concepts.) Then work directly with a contractor for construction. See Chapter 5.

- **Work with the architect AND contractor from the start.**
  Select an architect and a reputable contractor at the beginning of your project and work with both during the design process. An experienced contractor <u>may</u> be able to reduce construction costs by recommending cost effective building systems that can be incorporated into the plans. The contractor can estimate construction cost while plans are being prepared and develop a final bid price when they are complete. If for some reason you do not hire this contractor, you must pay for his or her time.

- **Find less expensive construction materials.**
  There are a few sources for "less than full cost" construction materials. Verify that your general contractor is willing to use these materials if you find them. Sources are:
  - Clearance, carload and suppliers' distress sales.
  - Suppliers' seconds are often good quality. Select carefully.
  - Purchase from the manufacturer. Some will sell directly to the public. (e.g. tile, floor covering).

- **Be your own general contractor.**
  If you act as the general contractor, you will hire each subcontractor (plumber, electrician, flooring contractor, cabinet maker, etc.) under a separate contract, and you are responsible for directing and coordinating their work. This may save up to 25% of cost of construction.

  CAUTION.....this is NOT AN EASY TASK if you have little or no knowledge of construction. It takes a lot of TIME and EFFORT, too. In addition, as a contractor and employer, you will also be required to carry Workers' Compensation and liability insurance and to file employer forms with the government.

  You may be able to hire less expensive labor if you act as general contractor. Students, retired craftspeople and individual construction workers might work for less if you hire them directly.

  Before deciding to take this route, review Chapter 7 on *Bidding and Contractor Selection,* research what contracting for residential construction includes or read a book on being your own general contractor. See books listed in the *Resources* section.

- **Do some construction work yourself.**
  If you have the experience and/or inclination, do some of the construction work yourself. You may save 10% to 40% of construction costs. Some tasks are relatively simple (for example, demolition, insulation installation, painting and daily clean-up) while others require more skill (plumbing and electrical work, installing wallboard and completing finish work). Other jobs are just frustrating and time consuming (taping and finishing wallboard) and not worth doing yourself.

  Many general contractors are willing to work with you on this basis, but it requires careful coordination and clearly defined (and written) responsibilities and liabilities. Remember, any work that you do should take your time, not the contractor's (do not bother the contractor with questions about how to do your job).

- **Do ALL of the construction work yourself.**
  You may be able to save 30% to 60% of construction costs by building yourself. There are many, many books available to help you. Some are listed in the *Resources*. However, it requires TIME, SKILL, EXPERIENCE, and PATIENCE.

Investment Target $

Evaluate these elements when you decide how much you want to invest.

Market Value of Homes in This Neighborhood

Recent selling prices of comparable homes. $—————

$—————

$—————

Recent selling prices of the best homes. $—————

$—————

$—————

Market value of this home before remodeling. $—————

Estimated Investment Recovery in One Year

Estimated construction cost for remodeling. $—————

Estimated recovery percentage.   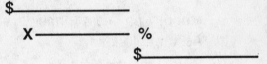 X————— %

Estimated investment recovery. $—————

Financing Available for the Project

Savings. $—————

Converting investments to cash. $—————

Borrowing money.

Home market value. $—————

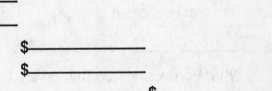 X   80 %

Amount lender will loan. $—————

Current mortgage amount. — $—————

Available to borrow. $—————

Other borrowing. $—————

Total financing available for this project. $—————

Amount I Am Willing to Spend on This Project    $—————

(What are my psychological spending limits?)

```
INVESTMENT TARGET
    CONSIDERING ALL OF THE ABOVE, MY
    INVESTMENT TARGET FOR THIS PROJECT IS:        $—————
```

$ Financing Checklist

Use this checklist to gather information from lenders and to learn what they need from you.

Lender _____   Date _____
Address _____   Loan Agent _____
_____   Phone _____

Amount of Loan Sought: $ _____

Terms of Loan.

Type of loan and rate: Fixed Rate _____ No. of years _____

Adjustable Rate _____ No. of years _____

(How often adjusted _____ Max._____ Min. _____)

Other _____

Monthly payment (principal + interest): $ _____
Assumable loan: Yes _____ No _____
Prepayment penalty: Yes _____ $ _____ No _____

Costs of the loan.

Points	$ _____	Prepaid interest	$ _____
Appraisal	$ _____	Loan insurance	$ _____
Title search	$ _____	Closing Fee	$ _____
Other	$ _____	Other	$ _____

Who is responsible for the title search? _____
How long does loan processing typically take? _____
Is there a cancellation charge? Yes _____ $ _____ No _____

What Forms and Information are Required?

Ask the lender for a copy of all forms you must complete and a list of all information you must provide. The lender may require the following:

- **Loan application form.**
- **Verification of Employment form**
    or Tax Returns and Financial Statements (if you are self-employed).
- **Verification of Deposit (from your bank/s).**
- **Copy of existing home fire insurance policy.**
- **Copies of floor plans for your remodeling.**
- **Other.**

Financing Checklist $

Use this checklist to gather information from lenders and to learn what they need from you.

Lender _____   Date _____

Address _____   Loan Agent _____

_____   Phone _____

Amount of Loan Sought: $ _____

Terms of Loan.

Type of loan and rate: Fixed Rate _____ No. of years _____

Adjustable Rate _____ No. of years _____

(How often adjusted _____ Max. _____ Min. _____)

Other _____

Monthly payment (principal + interest): $ _____

Assumable loan: Yes _____ No _____

Prepayment penalty: Yes _____ $ _____ No _____

Costs of the loan.

Points	$ _____	Prepaid interest	$ _____
Appraisal	$ _____	Loan insurance	$ _____
Title search	$ _____	Closing Fee	$ _____
Other	$ _____	Other	$ _____

Who is responsible for the title search? _____

How long does loan processing typically take? _____

Is there a cancellation charge?   Yes _____ $ _____ No _____

What Forms and Information are Required?

Ask the lender for a copy of all forms you must complete and a list of all information
you must provide. The lender may require the following:

• **Loan application form.**

• **Verification of Employment form**
   or Tax Returns and Financial Statements (if you are self-employed).

• **Verification of Deposit (from your bank/s).**

• **Copy of existing home fire insurance policy.**

• **Copies of floor plans for your remodeling.**

• **Other.**

$ Estimated Project Costs

	First Estimate	Modifications and Changes
Cost of Construction.		
New Construction _____ square feet		
X $_____ per sq ft =	$_____	$_____
Remodeled areas _____ square feet		
X $_____ per sq ft =	$_____	$_____
Kitchen	$_____	$_____
Bathroom	$_____	$_____
Other	$_____	$_____
Other	$_____	$_____
Subtotal Construction Cost	$_____	$_____

Consultant Fees

Construction cost $_____

Percent fees (15%-20%)   X_____%

(or less if you plan to

minimize consultant help)

Subtotal Fees	$_____	$_____

Permits and Reviews

Construction cost $_____

Percent permits (1.5%-2%)   X_____%

Subtotal Permits	$_____	$_____

Cost of Financing

Construction cost $_____

Percent financing (4%)   X_____%

Subtotal Financing	$_____	$_____

Cost of Furnishings

(As per needs.)

Subtotal Furnishings	$_____	$_____

Miscellaneous

Construction cost $_____

Percent misc. (15%-25%)   X_____%

Subtotal Miscellaneous	$_____	$_____

GRAND TOTAL PROJECT COSTS	$_____	$_____

DOES INVESTMENT TARGET EQUAL ESTIMATED PROJECT COSTS?

Actual Project Costs $

	Cost	Modifications
Cost of Construction	$_____	$_____
Consultant Fees	$_____	$_____
Architect	$_____	$_____
Interior Designer	$_____	$_____
Other	$_____	$_____
Other	$_____	$_____
Subtotal Consultants	$_____	$_____
Permits and Reviews		
Building Permit	$_____	$_____
Other_____	$_____	$_____
Other_____	$_____	$_____
Subtotal Permits	$_____	$_____
Cost of Financing		
Points	$_____	$_____
Appraisal	$_____	$_____
Title Search	$_____	$_____
Other_____	$_____	$_____
Subtotal Financing	$_____	$_____
Cost of Furnishings		
_____	$_____	$_____
_____	$_____	$_____
_____	$_____	$_____
Subtotal Furnishings	$_____	$_____
Miscellaneous		
Moving and rental	$_____	$_____
Change #1	$_____	$_____
Change #2	$_____	$_____
Change #3	$_____	$_____
Other_____	$_____	$_____
Subtotal Miscellaneous	$_____	$_____
ACTUAL PROJECT COSTS	$_____	$_____

4

ACTION.

WORKSHEETS.

✎ *Zoning.*
✎ *Planning.*
✎ *Building Codes.*

POTENTIAL PROBLEMS AND PITFALLS.

☛Community Building Regulations are designed to protect and help the public. You (or your designer or contractor) should try to understand the requirements of your particular department. If you don't understand what is required, trying to obtain information and permits is sometimes frustrating.Try to talk to the same department representative each time you ask questions and take notes about important interpretations.

☛When you investigate regulations, you may find that you are not allowed to make the changes that you want. Inquire about other solutions; you most likely will be able to solve your problem in another way.

☛Community review periods may add time to your project schedule. There is usually no way to shorten a standard review period. Ask how much time is required at the beginning of your project, plan for it and verify again later.

☛It is wise to ask if there are pending regulation changes that may affect your project. This does not happen often, but sometimes requirements change during the process.

Community Building Regulations

Before you begin designing your remodeling project, it is important to visit your Community Building Department to determine what local building regulations <u>require</u> and <u>allow</u>. Although you might expect that communities (cities or counties) require all construction to meet building safety codes, you may be surprised to learn that they also limit what and where you can build on your property. In addition, most communities require that you obtain a building permit before you begin any construction work, even interior remodeling. (There are exceptions. If you are doing cosmetic interior work like installing new flooring or new cabinets you may not need a permit. In any case, ask the Building Department.)

All communities have regulations, a combination of laws and ordinances, governing new construction and remodeling work for all buildings including homes. Their purpose is to protect the health and safety of the public and to guide community development according to approved plans. Community regulations typically have become more restrictive and more complex in recent years. For example, as we learn more about earthquakes, building codes require more complex structural design; or when neighborhoods become crowded, community planners limit additional growth in those areas. Regulations vary among communities.

Community building officials verify conformance to regulations in these ways:

1. Review proposed designs.

2. Approve plans for construction.

3. Issue permits for all construction work on your project. You must submit finished drawings, as defined by your community, to apply for a building permit. (Many communities require permits for demolition, too.)

4. Inspect the project at specific intervals during construction.

Types of Regulations

Regulations are usually divided into three groups - Zoning Ordinances, Planning Regulations and Building Codes:

Zoning Ordinances

Zoning ordinances define how land can be used throughout the community (a variety of residential, commercial, industrial and public use zones) and establish boundaries between different zones. They also regulate use within each zone, maximum building size and where buildings can be located on each lot. In residential zones your community may regulate the following:

- Distance from property lines to buildings. (Setbacks).
- Maximum building height and number of stories.
- Fence locations and heights.
- Off street parking requirements. (Often a garage and driveway parking spaces are required.)
- Allowable lot coverage. (You can build on a defined maximum percent of your property.)
- Business use. (Some home businesses are allowed in residential zones.)

See the sketches in this chapter that illustrate examples of zoning requirements.

Planning Regulations

Planning regulations usually apply to enforcement of your community general plan for development. They may relate to:

- Building appearance. (Architectural Review.)
- Environmental impact of the building.
- Preservation of historic structures.
- Construction moratoriums. (A period during which construction is limited and the community plan is being evaluated or revised.)

Building Codes

Building codes govern construction practices - how a building should be built and what materials may be used. Their goals include making certain that your home is safe for you and the community. They define standards for all parts of a building including:

- Foundations.
- Floor, wall and roof framing.
- Electrical service and wiring.
- Sanitation, plumbing fixtures and pipes.
- Heating systems and ducts.
- Ventilation.
- Roof and wall finish materials.
- Energy conservation requirements (insulation, limits for total area of windows, etc.)
- Fire safety.

In addition, if you are making major changes in an older home, the Building Department may require you to upgrade the entire building to meet current building codes. This usually applies only if the cost of the remodeling is greater than or equal to 50% of the market value of the existing house (excluding the land), but it is wise to ask.

Visiting the Building Department

The titles of community building departments vary, and sometimes Zoning, Planning and Building Codes are managed by separate departments. Start your investigation with "Building Inspection", the "Building Department" or the "Building Division". (Call "Information" at City Hall if no building department is listed in the telephone directory.) If this department can not answer all your questions, they can direct you to the appropriate locations.

Keep in mind that the purpose of your visit is to learn about general requirements that affect the design of your remodeling. The architect or contractor will ask detailed questions about construction requirements and apply for permits later. Typically the architect or contractor investigates all community building regulations and provides information to satisfy approvals, permits and inspections. But you will gain a basic understanding of the requirements, the process and the people if you do some preliminary investigation yourself. Use the worksheets in this chapter to ask questions about *Zoning, Planning and Building Codes*. Some questions may not apply to your project.

Talking to the Department Representatives

When you talk to the department representatives, identify yourself, describe your proposed project and its location, ask questions such as those provided on the worksheets and inquire about the general regulations that apply to your project. Take rough sketches or existing plans if you have them. (Some building departments have prepared handouts describing requirements for homes. Obtain a copy if your building department has one.)

If you learn that your ideas for remodeling will not meet the regulations, find out if there is something similar that will be acceptable. Ask all the questions that have occurred to you; it may save you another trip to the department. Also find out if there are changes anticipated in the regulations that might impact your project, and when the changes are likely to become effective. Finally, write down the names and phone numbers of the people you talk to in case you have further questions.

You may find that building department representatives are used to dealing with architects and contractors who are familiar with construction regulations and terminology. If you do not understand what they tell you, do not hesitate to ask them to explain further.

It is important to remember that these departments interpret community building regulations. Every possible combination of circumstances cannot be written down. Department representatives talk to many people every day about a wide variety of situations. Sometimes different representatives will interpret the same question in different ways, and sometimes even the same representative may give different interpretations of similar questions at two separate times. Write down what each person tells you. If the interpretation is very important to your project, send a memo of your conversation to the representative for the records. Be sure to bring your notes if you return to ask more questions.

A last word about talking to the building department: it is VERY helpful for you and/or your architect and contractor to create and maintain a good working relationship with your community building representatives. Once you have found someone who answers your questions, talk to the same person, if possible, with subsequent questions to maintain continuity. He or she is likely to remember your project. If you talk to several different people, write down all their names and maintain a good working relationship with each person. However, do not be afraid to ask for the head building official if you feel that the department representatives are not giving you complete explanations.

There will be fewer problems if you find out requirements early. If problems occur, they will be easier to resolve with people who know you and your project in a favorable light.

Variances

If existing regulations will not allow you to make the changes that you want, your community <u>may</u> grant a "variance" or exception to the regulations for your project. A variance most often is granted in a hardship situation, not just because you want it. The department representative can tell you about the application procedure. Typically, you must complete a written application, pay a fee and submit drawings to a reviewing group (and/or public meeting) showing your proposed change. The process varies among communities and sometimes it is time consuming and complex. Ask the representative if your variance is likely to be granted; he or she usually knows what is apt to be acceptable. It may save some time and effort.

Reviews, Approvals and Permits

Ask which reviews, approvals and permits are required for your project and find out what information must be submitted. (Be certain to ask how much time is needed for review, because review periods may add weeks to your time schedule.) Typically you will need only a building permit, but you may need additional subpermits for plumbing, heating and cooling and electrical work. The general contractor will apply for the necessary permits when he is ready to begin construction.

If you do not obtain a building permit, your community may charge a penalty fee or require completed construction to be uncovered for inspection. Furthermore, construction work done without a permit may cause problems when you sell or refinance your home. In California, for example, a recent law requires that home sellers make available to buyers a "seller transfer disclosure statement", a detailed list about the condition and integrity of a house. Work done without a permit may require inspection and reconstruction. ∎

Example of Zoning Requirements

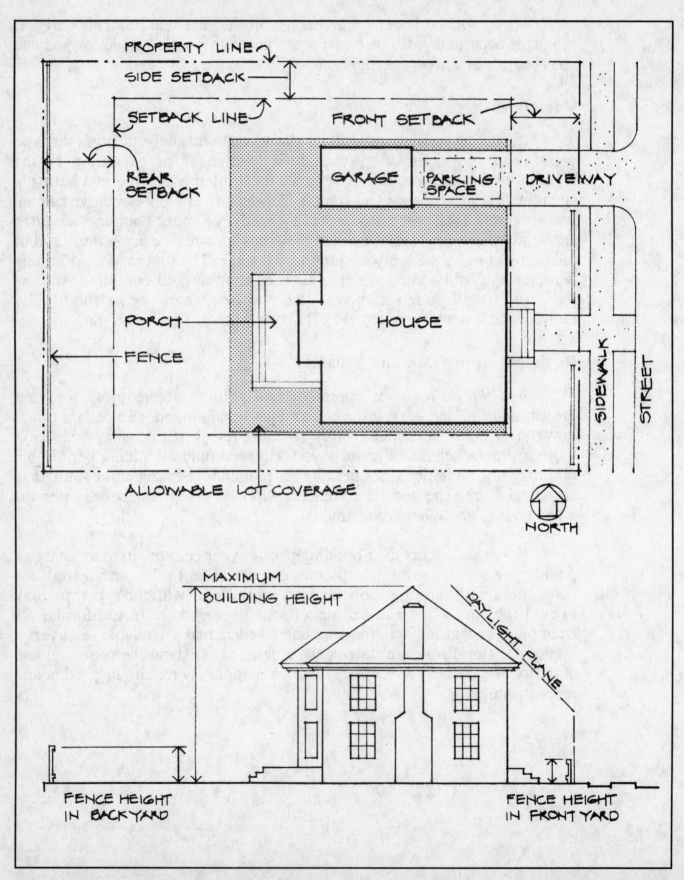

Zoning

Date _____

Some questions may not apply, especially for interior remodeling.

City/County _____   **Department** _____

Project Address _____   Dept. Address _____

_____   _____

Talked to _____   Phone No. _____

Do you have a written handout or pamphlet of residential zoning requirements? _____

What zone is my house in? _____   What does this zone allow? _____

_____

Minimum Lot Size:

Area _____ sq.ft.   or   Lot size _____ ft. X _____ ft.

What is the allowable lot coverage? (I can build on _____ % of my property.)

Building Setbacks from Property Lines:

Front Setback _____ ft.   Rear Setback _____ ft.

Side Setback _____ ft.   Side Setback _____ ft.

Are second story setbacks same as first? Yes _____ No _____ _____ ft.

Can roof eaves overhang into setbacks? Yes _____ No _____

If so, how far at front? _____ ft.   Rear? _____ ft.   Side? _____ ft.

Where is front property line in relationship to street or sidewalk? (Property may start a

few feet behind edge of street or sidewalk.) _____

Fences:

Allowed height in front setback. _____   Allowed height on rest of property. _____

Detached garages and accessory buildings (shed, greenhouse, etc.):

Front Setback _____ ft. Rear _____ ft. Side _____ ft.

Other Requirements _____

Building Height:

Maximum height _____ ft.   Number of stories permitted _____

Are there "daylight plane" requirements? (Does your house have to slope away from

the property line at a required angle to allow sunlight into neighboring yards?) _____

Off-street Parking Requirements:

Garage: Yes _____ No _____   How many cars? _____

Is a carport allowed instead of a garage?   Yes _____   No _____

Is other uncovered off-street parking required? Yes ___ No ___ How many cars? ___

Variance Procedure (if a change is desired):

What information is needed? _____

How many copies? _____ Fee $ _____ When to submit? _____

Who reviews? _____ How long does review take? _____

Are any changes planned for residential zones in the near future? Yes _____ No _____

Notes

Planning

Date _____

Some questions may not apply.

City/County _____   **Department** _____

Project Address _____   Dept. Address _____

_____   _____

Talked to _____   Phone No. _____

Do you have a written handout or pamphlet of residential requirements? _____

Is Architectural Review Required?   Yes _____   No _____

    What information is needed?   _____

    _____

    How many copies? _____   Fee $ _____   When to submit? _____

    Who reviews? _____   How long does review take? _____

    Is there a review meeting I should attend? _____

Is an Environmental Impact Statement (EIS) or Environmental Impact Report (EIR) Required?

                              Yes _____   No _____

    What information is needed?   _____

    _____

    How many copies? _____   Fee $ _____   When to submit? _____

    Who reviews? _____   How long does review take? _____

    Is there a review meeting I should attend? _____

Is My Home in a Historic Preservation District?   Yes _____   No _____

    If so, what are the requirements that affect my house? _____

_____

_____

Other:

    Can I remove trees from my lot?   Yes _____   No _____

    Other

_____

_____

_____

Are any changes planned for residential areas in the near future? Yes _____   No _____

    What? _____

    When? _____

Notes

Building Codes

Date _____

Some questions may not apply.

City/County _____ **Department** _____

Project Address _____ Dept. Address _____

_____ _____

Talked to _____ Phone No. _____

Do you have a written handout or pamphlet of requirements for residential construction?_____

What Building Codes are now in use? _____

_____

Building Permit Requirements: (Ask for a copy of the application form.)

What plans must be submitted?   What scale? _____

    Site or Plot Plan _____   Exterior Elevations _____

    Floor Plans _____   Roof Plan _____

    Foundation Plans _____   Plumbing, Heating and/or _____

    Framing Plans _____   Electrical Plans _____

    Other _____   Other _____

What information must appear on the plans? _____

_____

How many copies of plans must be submitted?_____

Will any part of the existing structure need to be brought up to current building code

standards?   Yes _____ No _____ What? _____

_____

Are energy calculations required? Yes _____ No _____   What does this include?

    (Ask for a copy of the calculation form.) _____

How much is building permit fee? $ _____ Is there a plan check fee? $ _____

How long does it take to get a building permit?_____

What are the penalties if I do not get a permit? _____

If you are considering an extensive project or thinking about adding a second story, ask:

    Are structural calculations required? Yes _____ No _____   How many copies? _____

    Is a soil test required?   Yes _____ No _____

    Is a sewer permit required?   Yes _____ No _____

Other

If you have a septic system and plan to add a bathroom/s, ask:

    Is a percolation test required?   Yes _____ No _____

Do I need an "Occupancy Permit" before I can move into the new and remodeled rooms?

                                Yes _____ No _____

Are any changes planned for residential areas in the near future?

    What? _____   When? _____

5

ACTION.

POTENTIAL PROBLEMS AND PITFALLS.

☛ It is important to select a design consultant who has appropriate experience for your project and who will listen to you. If you feel that you have made a mistake, it is always possible to select a different designer.

☛ Be sure that you understand what services the designer will provide for your project. Do not make assumptions.

☛ SIGN A CONTRACT WITH THE DESIGNER BEFORE HE OR SHE STARTS WORK. There will be less chance for misunderstanding.

Design Consultants

At this point you will be anxious to begin making specific plans for your project. Your ideas must be transformed into construction drawings which are two dimensional plans drawn to scale. You will need to have construction drawings (often called simply drawings or plans) for three reasons:

- To secure a building permit.
- To obtain contractors' bids for construction.
- To serve as the basis from which to build.

Before you go any further, you should consider whether or not you want to hire a design consultant to help with plans for your remodeling project.

Do You Need a Design Consultant?

Most homeowners need some assistance to transform ideas into construction drawings. Many hire an architect or another designer to prepare plans, although some homeowners are able to draw their own plans. (Generally communities do not require that a licensed professional prepare the plans for a single family residence.) A rule of thumb is that if your project will cost more than $25,000 (for example, you are making major changes like completely redesigning the kitchen or adding a second story), it is probably best to work with an experienced design consultant such as an architect or a building designer, or an interior designer for interior changes and furniture selection. He or she can interpret your needs and give you alternative designs (there is always more than one solution) for attractive functional rooms. Most designers will structure their services to meet the needs of a large or small remodeling project.

If you know exactly what you want and your design ideas are very straight-forward (they will not involve major structural changes), you may want to hire a draftsperson to draw the plans. Another alternative is to work directly with the general contractor who will build your project. Sometimes contractors prepare the plans that you need for permits. (See Chapter 7 for a discussion of contractors.)

Types of Design Consultants

The following paragraphs outline some of the basic differences among the categories of design conslutants. Keep in mind that there are differences within each category, too. For example, all architects do not have the same design skills or knowledge of building systems just as all doctors do not offer exactly the same medical services. Think about which professional will be right for your project.

Architect.

An architect is a professional designer who is trained to consider all dimensions of a project - the users' functional needs, the aesthetics and the engineering requirements. He or she typically has a college degree in architecture, has worked for three or more years as an apprentice and then has earned a license from the state by passing a rigorous examination. Many, but not all, licensed architects belong to the American Institute of Architects (AIA) and indicate "AIA" after their names. The AIA is a professional organization and membership is voluntary.

An architect can provide these services:

- Prepare alternative design concepts (schematic designs) for remodeling existing rooms or adding new rooms.
- Make certain that your project meets building codes and ordinances.
- Help estimate costs.
- Make recommendations for materials, fixtures, lighting, appliances and colors.
- Prepare complete construction drawings and specifications including details for special architectural features like cabinets, window trim, ceiling molding and others.
- Manage the bidding/negotiation with contractors.
- Manage contract administration (make regular visits to the project during construction to answer questions and solve problems).

An architect will work with you from planning through design and construction. He or she can consolidate your remodeling ideas into a cohesive plan. Many also help select furnishings, but an interior designer typically will have more expertise in that area. Architects may hire other consultants for structural or electrical design or energy analysis.

Building Designer.

Building designers often have training much like architects, but may have less formal education. They are usually licensed by the state, too. If a building designer has two years of architecture or building technology training, six years of work experience for a licensed designer and passes a professional exam, the American Institute of Building Designers allows the use of "AIBD" after his or her name. Building designers can provide many of the same services that architects provide.

Specialized Designer.

Some specialized contractors or retail stores offer design/build services for kitchens and bathrooms. They not only will design your kitchen or bathroom remodeling, but they also will build it with the types of cabinets that they sell or make. These designers come from different backgrounds that may include design training and/or construction experience. The design fees are usually included with construction costs.

Interior Designer.

Interior designers most often redesign existing rooms or work with an architect to design interiors for new rooms. They have a variety of backgrounds: many have design school degrees and years of experience, while others have learned the design business through experience alone. There are no formal licensing requirements for interior designers at this time, but that may change soon. If a designer belongs to the American Society of Interior Designers, he or she has passed that organization's professional exam and may indicate "ASID" after his or her name.

Interior designers are trained to consider interior functions, the appearance and character of rooms and selection of furniture, finishes, fabrics, lighting and accessories. Depending on background and experience, interior designers may be able to design entire rooms (including storage and cabinets) or may limit themselves to furnishings, finishes and colors. Interior designers can provide drawings for interior work, but if structural changes are involved, make certain that a qualified person (engineer or architect) has designed the structural work.

If you want to work with both an architect and an interior designer, it is helpful to select both professionals at the beginning of your project so they can coordinate their design efforts throughout. It is also important to make certain that these individuals can work together with respect and good communication.

The following two consultants can prepare plans but it is not likely that they will have strong design skills.

Draftsperson.

A draftsperson has technical training to draw plans, but he or she may not have training for design or structural work. There are no formal requirements to be a draftsperson. A draftsperson can produce plans from which you can obtain contractors' bids and building permits.

General Contractor.

If you know the name of a good general contractor (one who has satisfied clients among your friends and has been given excellent recommendations), you may want to hire him or her to build your remodeling project without obtaining competitive bids. This contractor may be able to take your design ideas and produce plans for obtaining building permits. But since a contractor's primary expertise is construction, he or she may need a draftsperson to draw plans.

Finding a Design Consultant

You may know exactly who you want to hire, but if not, collect names of possible design consultants. Use the *Names of Designers* form in this chapter for your list. There are a number of sources.

- Friends and business acquaintances.
- The "Home" section of your local newspaper, home magazines and home design books. (Local designers are usually the most convenient.)
- Remodeling projects that you see and like. (Ask the owner who designed it.)
- American Institute of Architects (AIA) (Contact the local office for architects' names).
- American Society of Interior Designers (ASID) (Contact the local office for interior designers' names).
- Real estate agents.
- The Yellow Pages of your telephone directory.

(This is a last resort. Many architects and firms listed in the Yellow Pages do not design residential remodelings; they design commercial projects. It is generally impossible to know because most architects do not advertise their specialities.)

Note: The AIA and the ASID maintain lists of residential designers. When you call, they will give you a few names in your area, but you will not be given specific recommendations for one designer versus another.

After you assemble a list of names, make preliminary phone calls, describe your project including your budget and ask the following:

- Is the designer interested in designing your project?
- Does the designer normally design projects like yours?
- Ask the designer to describe similar work.
- Ask the designer to describe the firm's, his or her individual background, whichever is appropriate.
- Can the designer meet your schedule for completing drawings?

The answers to these questions should enable you to select three or four designers to interview in-person.

Selecting a Design Consultant

Set up interviews. Meet the designers, discuss your project and budget further and see examples of their work (either review photographs or visit specific projects). Use the *Designer Selection* worksheet to record information. Ask for references and permission to call them. The *Questions for Designers' Clients* worksheet will be helpful when you check the references.

Making a final selection is sometimes difficult. Remodeling your home is on one hand a technical process and on the other hand a very personal experience. Your home is a retreat and a special place for you and your family. When you select a design consultant, you want to choose someone who has not only experience and technical expertise, but also the ability to understand and interpret your needs. Think about the following criteria when you evaluate designers.

Experience.
If a designer has experience with home remodeling projects similar to yours, he or she will understand the complexity, the design problems,

the materials and the budget considerations. In general, designers' technical skills increase with experience, but if a designer has a license, you know that he or she has the experience required to pass state qualifying exams.

It is also important to select a designer whose past work you like. You should have a positive response to his or her portfolio of projects. Most designers tend to have a certain style and feeling to their work. This does not mean, however, that all their projects will look alike. But if you like clean and simple contemporary lines, it is a good idea to select a designer whose work demonstrates this; if you like traditional or historic styles, select someone who has worked with them before.

Experience with projects in your community is an asset for your designer, but it is not essential. As stated earlier, each community has widely varied regulations and requirements for building. If the designer has worked in your community before, he or she knows the process.

Performance.
Talk with a designer's client references. Ask if the designer met schedule and budget requirements, did satisfactory design work, completed drawings as per contract and worked cooperatively with client and contractor. Good recommendations are very important when you hire professionals to help with your remodeling.

Communication and responsiveness.
You and your family should be able to communicate EASILY with your designer and feel comfortable with him or her. It is important to select someone who will listen to you because that person must translate your particular family needs into attractive functional spaces. Remember, you are the person who will live with the final design, not the designer. The designer must be able to listen and interpret what you want. Of course you should listen to your designer's recommendations (he or she has the design skills and experience) and carefully evaluate what is proposed.

Capacity and capability.
Make certain that the designer you select will have the time for your project to meet your overall schedule. If you are talking to a design firm rather than an individual, ask who will be working on your project. Usually a firm owner interviews for new work, but other

people in the firm perform much of the work. If another person will be managing your remodeling, ask to meet that person.

Fees.
Sometimes professional design fees are an important factor in selecting a designer. However, if you really like a designer, there is usually a way to work out a fee that will fit your budget. Review the next section, *The Contract Between You and Your Designer*.

The Contract Between You and Your Designer

Before your designer begins work, you must agree on the specific work tasks to be done and the design fees. THERE SHOULD BE A WRITTEN CONTRACT BETWEEN YOU AND EACH PROFESSIONAL THAT YOU EMPLOY TO DO DESIGN WORK OR CONSULTATION ON YOUR HOME REMODELING PROJECT. It is important to know exactly what you are getting for your money. A good contract helps prevent problems, and there is less chance for misunderstanding if the responsibilities of BOTH the designer and the owner are written down at the beginning.

A contract may be a single page that outlines the designer's work tasks, owner's responsiblities, schedule, amount of fee and payment method, or it may be a several page document. Most designers will propose using a standard contract form. Architects, for example, often use contracts prepared by the American Institute of Architects. Make certain that you understand everything in the contract. Also before you sign anything, it is wise to consult your legal counsel.

Design Work Tasks.
Your designer will present and explain a list of the work tasks that he or she can perform. You can ask the designer to show you examples of the type of plans he or she will prepare, too, so that you will know how much detail to expect. Then you and the designer determine a final list of tasks which will both meet your budget and achieve your project goals. Although most designers prefer to work on the entire project from design and preparation of drawings through administering the construction contract between the owner and the general contractor, many are willing to assist with projects on a limited basis. For example, if you want to minimize design fees, you may want to hire a designer to prepare alternative design concepts and outline specifications for your project. Then employ a draftsperson to prepare final plans based on the design concept you select. Another alternative is to hire a designer to prepare design and construction drawings only.

You can oversee construction yourself and employ the designer on an hourly basis when necessary for special questions.

Design Fees.

Your contract should state the amount of design fees and the terms of payment by the owner to the designer. There are several ways to arrange billing of design fees. Most designers will have a preference for a particular method and most will invoice on a monthly basis rather than after the job is complete. In addition, most designers will ask for reimbursable expenses such as cost of making construction drawing prints and cost of long distance travel and communications. (Use the *Payments to the Designer* form to keep track of invoices and payments.) See the section on *How Designers Bill Fees* for more detail. Also include a statement about how fees will be determined if you should want the designer to do work not included in the original contract.

If you stop the design process or decide not to build the project, you must pay the designer for the work that he or she has completed.

In addition to a description of work tasks and fees, it is a good idea to include an arbitration clause (a statement providing that disputes may be settled by an arbitrator) and a statement about contract termination if either party feels that the relationship should cease. Typically architects will include a statement saying that they retain ownership of drawings, that is, you may keep reference copies for yourself but you can not use them again or sell them without the architect's permission. Use the checklist for *Contract between Owner and Designer* to help establish the content of your contract. ∎

The following list shows some of the most common billing methods used by designers:

• Hourly Billing Rate (Time and Materials).
Design consultants charge a wide range of rates ($30-$120 per hour) depending on their experience and expertise and depending on who in the firm (a senior or junior person) works on the project. This method is open-ended and is the most difficult to estimate at the outset of the project. However, if you need only a few hours of consultation, this can be a reasonable payment method.

• Hourly Billing Rate with a Target Maximum.
This method is based on hourly rates but sets a maximum fee limitation. You and your designer agree on work tasks and a maximum fee. Then the designer completes the work tasks and bills at the agreed upon rates. You may be billed less than the maximum, but you will not be billed more than the maximum for the agreed upon work.

• Lump Sum or Stipulated Sum Fee (Flat rate).
If you select the lump sum fee method, you will pay an agreed upon amount for the design work that you want done. The designer bases the lump sum fee on the outlined work. You will be billed the same amount for the work no matter how much time the designer spends.

• Percentage of Construction Cost.
This method sets the fee in relation to the cost of construction. If the construction cost increases over the original estimate, the designer will receive a larger fee than initially estimated and vice versa.

• Combination of Hourly Rate and Lump Sum.
Sometimes it is best to use a combination of payment methods. If you are considering a project with a wide range of variables, it may be a good idea to work on an hourly basis (with or without a maximum) through the preliminary design phase until the project is more specifically defined. Then you can agree upon a lump sum (or percentage of construction cost) to complete the project.

• Fees for Additional Services.
If you request your architect to do work which was not described in your original agreement, he or she may ask for additional fees. Additional fees are often billed on an hourly basis.

Names of Designers

NAME and FIRM	PHONE	SOURCE	COMMENT
1 _____ _____	_____	_____	_____ _____
2 _____ _____	_____	_____	_____
3 _____ _____	_____	_____	_____
4 _____ _____	_____	_____	_____
5 _____ _____	_____	_____	_____
6 _____ _____	_____	_____	_____
7 _____ _____	_____	_____	_____
8 _____ _____	_____	_____	_____

QUESTIONS TO ASK DESIGNERS

Call the designers on your list, describe your project including your budget and ask the following questions.

1. Are you interested in doing the design work and necessary drawings on this project?
2. Have you designed projects like this before and do you currently work on projects like this?
3. Describe some of your work/similar projects.
4. Describe your firm's background (if appropriate).
5. I would like to start building in _____ (what month), will my project fit into your schedule?

Designer Selection

Date _____

Firm _____   Representative _____

Address _____   Phone No. _____

_____   Recommended by _____

My Project is: _____   My Budget is: $_____

Experience:

How many similar projects have you designed? _____

Examples _____

_____

How long in business? _____   How many employees ? _____

Are you licensed in this state?   Yes _____   No _____

Have you worked in my community before?   Yes _____   No _____

Who will be working on my project? _____

Will my project fit into your work schedule?   Yes _____   No _____

When can you start work? _____

Approximately how long will plans take? _____

References:

Client _____   Client _____

Address _____   Address _____

_____   _____

Phone _____   Phone _____

Comments _____   Comments _____

_____   _____

Client _____   Client _____

Address _____   Address _____

_____   _____

Phone _____   Phone _____

Comments _____   Comments _____

_____   _____

Fee Structure:

Can you give me a rough estimate of what your fees might be for my project? $ _____

How do you typically bill a client for services? (Type of contact, how often.) _____

My Evaluation:

Experience. _____

Performance. _____

Communication and Responsiveness _____

Capacity and Capability. _____

Questions for Designers' Clients

1. Were you satisfied with the work of this designer?

2. Did the designer provide a creative solution for your remodeling problem?
   Was the designer responsive to your needs?

3. Did the Final Project Cost meet your Budget Target?
   If not, by what percentage was the project over budget?
   Were you satisfied with the information you received about cost during
   the design process?

4. Did the designer meet your schedule for completing plans?

5. Did you enjoy working with the designer on a day-to-day basis?

6. Did the designer work well with the contractor and others involved in the project?

7. WOULD YOU HIRE THE DESIGNER AGAIN?

Designer Selection

Date _____

Firm _____   Representative _____

Address _____   Phone No. _____

_____   Recommended by _____

My Project is: _____   My Budget is: $_____

Experience:

How many similar projects have you designed? _____

Examples _____

_____

How long in business? _____   How many employees ?_____

Are you licensed in this state?   Yes _____   No _____

Have you worked in my community before?   Yes _____   No _____

Who will be working on my project?   _____

Will my project fit into your work schedule? Yes _____   No _____

When can you start work?   _____

Approximately how long will plans take?   _____

References:

Client _____   Client _____

Address _____   Address _____

_____   _____

Phone _____   Phone _____

Comments _____   Comments _____

_____   _____

Client _____   Client _____

Address _____   Address _____

_____   _____

Phone _____   Phone _____

Comments _____   Comments _____

_____   _____

Fee Structure:

Can you give me a rough estimate of what your fees might be for my project? $ _____

How do you typically bill a client for services? (Type of contact, how often.) _____

My Evaluation:

Experience. _____

Performance._____

Communication and Responsiveness_____

Capacity and Capability._____

Questions for Designers' Clients

1. Were you satisfied with the work of this designer?

2. Did the designer provide a creative solution for your remodeling problem?
   Was the designer responsive to your needs?

3. Did the Final Project Cost meet your Budget Target?
   If not, by what percentage was the project over budget?
   Were you satisfied with the information you received about cost during
   the design process?

4. Did the designer meet your schedule for completing plans?

5. Did you enjoy working with the designer on a day-to-day basis?

6. Did the designer work well with the contractor and others involved in the project?

7. WOULD YOU HIRE THE DESIGNER AGAIN?

Contract Between Owner and Designer
Checklist

The following are some of the items that should appear in your contract with a designer.

- **Owner name and address.**
- **Architect/Designer name and address.**
- **Description of the project.**
- **Architect/Designer responsibilities.**
   (Include a specific list of the services/tasks that you want the designer to do. Some
   general services are listed below.)
   - Record existing conditions.
   - Produce written program or summary of design criteria.
   - Provide design alternatives.
   - Produce plans and specifications.
   - Assist with Bid/Negotiation.
   - Manage Construction Administration.
   - Other.
- **Owner responsibilities.**
   - Provide Program information.
   - Provide Budget information.
   - Site Survey } If necessary for a difficult site, the owner
   - Soil Report } usually hires these consultants directly.
   - Timely information and decisions.
   - Other.
- **Estimated time schedule.**
- **Contract payment amount and description of reimbursable expenses.**
- **Terms of payment by owner to architect/designer.** (Will the designer be paid a percentage,
   by the hour, etc. and will the designer invoice monthly, by phase, etc.?)
- **Provision for additional services.**   (How will the designer be paid if the owner wants
   additional work not outlined in the contract?)
- **Arbitration clause.**
- **Provisions for termination of agreement.**

Note: Before you sign any contract, it is wise to consult your legal counsel.

Payments to the Designer

TOTAL CONTRACT AMOUNT $_____

ADDITIONAL SERVICES $_____

     $_____

Payment No.	Date	Payment Amount	Paid to Date	Amount Remaining
_____	__/__/__	$_____	$_____	$_____
_____	__/__/__	$_____	$_____	$_____
_____	__/__/__	$_____	$_____	$_____
_____	__/__/__	$_____	$_____	$_____
_____	__/__/__	$_____	$_____	$_____
_____	__/__/__	$_____	$_____	$_____
_____	__/__/__	$_____	$_____	$_____
_____	__/__/__	$_____	$_____	$_____
		Total Paid	$_____	

REIMBURSABLES

Payment No.	Date	Payment Amount	Paid to Date
_____	__/__/__	$_____	$_____
_____	__/__/__	$_____	$_____
_____	__/__/__	$_____	$_____
_____	__/__/__	$_____	$_____
_____	__/__/__	$_____	$_____
_____	__/__/__	$_____	$_____
_____	__/__/__	$_____	$_____
_____	__/__/__	$_____	$_____
		Total Paid	$_____

TOTAL PAYMENTS TO DESIGNER $_____

6

ACTION.

WORKSHEETS.

POTENTIAL PROBLEMS AND PITFALLS.

☛During design, it is easy to add details that may increase building cost (more built-in cabinets, expensive finishes, a little more area, etc.) Be aware of the potential for increasing cost when you make decisions about details of the project. This is a point where you can lose control of your budget.

☛Be sure to allow time during design for community reviews, if they are required.

The Design Process

After you have gathered background information and decided if you want to hire a design consultant, you will begin to develop the actual plans for your project. This design process involves finding a solution that will satisfy your needs, budget requirements and community building regulations; selecting materials and deciding about details; and producing final construction drawings. If you work with a design professional, the process will probably be divided into specific phases similar to those explained below. Whether you work with a designer or not, you will go through the same type of development to finalize your plans.

You will make numerous decisions during the design process. There are many small details (light switch plates, molding and cabinet hinges) as well as larger more obvious items (flooring, window style and wall materials) that you may want to select at this time. Do not be overwhelmed by the quantity of possible decisions; many will require very little thought. The checklists and worksheets in this chapter outline design decisions which you may need to make, but some may not apply to your project. Typically your designer will make recommendations and help you with all the decisions. Spend extra time only on those decisions which are really important to you.

There are also some *Design Meeting Memo* forms at the end of this chapter. Use them during the design process to keep track of decisions, deadlines and responsibilities.

Predesign

Before your designer puts pencil to paper, he or she will want to know more about your remodeling goals, your existing home and your tastes in design. Your designer will record this information and may prepare a "program" or written summary to use as a guide during design.

Reviewing Your Remodeling Goals

Review your needs, goals, priorities, room analysis and budget plans with the designer and relate anything you have learned about your community building regulations. If you have used the forms in this workbook, you may want to copy appropriate ones for the designer. Your organized beginning will save time and help the design process proceed efficiently. Also discuss your proposed project schedule.

Collecting Information About Your Existing House and Property

The designer must document your existing house (or the part that you want to remodel) before he or she can prepare plans for changes:

- The designer will visit your home, see the spaces that you want to remodel and may take reference photographs of existing conditions.

- The designer needs floor plans of the existing rooms as a basis from which to work. If you have prints or plans of your house, the designer can use them. If you have made careful base plans, the designer will verify them. If not, he or she will measure the rooms and draw the existing plans. The designer also may measure the entire perimeter of your house and prepare a site plan or plot plan showing the location of the house on the property. Many communities require you to submit a site plan to obtain a building permit. The designer also will want to know the legal description of your property (from your deed) and any restrictions or easements which would affect the design.

  In addition, the designer will record information about the structural, plumbing and electrical work that may need to be changed. Since much of this work is concealed inside walls, assumptions are often made.

- Then the designer will visit your community Building Department to investigate community regulations or verify information that you researched.

Describe Your Tastes in Design and Style

Your designer will want to know how you envision your remodeled spaces (for example, modern, traditional, light and airy, dark and cozy) and what you like and dislike in design. He or she may have a specific format to collect this information, but you also can use the *Design Tastes* worksheet to record your preferences. The designer will use your ideas in a creative way to solve your design problems. He or she may propose something very different from what you envisioned, but consistent with your tastes and goals.

Some good ways to help organize your thoughts include:

- Select photographs from books and magazines which show houses, rooms or specific details that you like (hardwood floors, windows with small panes, track lighting or a special sink). Pick some rooms that evoke a positive response for you even if they are not what you imagined for your own home. Also select a few which illustrate rooms you do not like.

- Tour your community and look for homes that you find attractive, walk through model homes and visit your neighbors' homes. In many communities, charitable organizations sponsor "Decorator Show House" tours as benefits. Decorator Show Houses are large homes that have been renovated and decorated by a group of interior designers and usually show a wide variety of design styles. Tours are often in the spring.

- Visit kitchen and bath shops. Most communities have shops where you can see examples of cabinets, review plan layouts and examine samples of fixtures and hardware. Often they will give you design catalogs and brochures.

- Look at furnishings in furniture showrooms. They can be a resource to help you define design ideas. The furnishings you ultimately select play a major part in determining the style and character of your remodeled rooms.

Preliminary or Schematic Design

After the designer has collected enough background information, he or she will begin to prepare plans. During this phase of design the basic plan solution for your home remodeling project will be developed.

Preparing Preliminary Plans

First the designer will prepare sketches showing one or more alternatives for your home remodeling project. They may include:

- Site plan.
- Floor plans (often showing furniture).
- Elevations.
- Suggested building materials.
- Suggested colors.

Then review the alternative plans with the designer, evaluate them and select a design direction. The design direction establishes the basic floor plan (build one story versus two; remove walls rather than add space; convert the garage rather than the basement, etc.) When you evaluate the alternatives, think about the following:

- Traffic flow.
- Size and shape of rooms.
- Use of rooms.
- Windows and skylights.
- Exterior design.

Refer to the *Plan Review Checklist* in this chapter for additional evaluation criteria. It is important that you understand the plans thoroughly when you select a design direction. If you have trouble visualizing or understanding the design sketches, ask your designer to clarify the concepts with more explanation or additional sketches. Although you can always make changes later, your designer may require more compensation if you change to a completely different design direction when drawings are almost complete.

After you select a design direction, the designer will refine the plans and draw your project in more detail. He or she also may prepare a perspective sketch or study model (rough small scale model built of artists' construction board) to help illustrate the design.

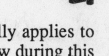

If your community requires architectural review (typically applies to exterior changes only), your project will be submitted for review during this phase. The designer will prepare the necessary drawings. If the reviewing agency requires changes, the changes must be made at this time.

Developing a Preliminary Cost Estimate

Many designers will help develop a preliminary cost estimate for construction (statement of probable construction cost) based on the preliminary plans. The estimate may be prepared by the designer, a cost estimating consultant or a general contractor. It will help indicate whether or not you are meeting your budget target. Use the *Preliminary Cost Estimate* and the *Construction Cost Estimate Divisions* worksheets for notes when your designer reviews the estimate with you. If the estimated costs exceed your budget, consider making trade-offs and modifying your plans to achieve BOTH your design and budget goals. (Refer to *Ways to Save Money* in Chapter 3 and *Cost Cutting Checklist* in Chapter 7.)

An important thing to remember is that this is a <u>preliminary</u> cost estimate. During this stage, the cost estimator must make some assumptions about the finished product. If you decide on expensive materials, expand the project or make other changes during the next stage, this cost estimate may be too low. (Sometimes the designer will add a 10% to 15% design contingency to the preliminary estimate in anticipation of these changes.)

Considering Furnishings

It is also important to consider furnishings during the first phases of design. The furnishings that you choose (or own) will affect the flow of traffic through rooms, room shape and size, location and size of doors and windows and selection of colors and materials. Do you want large over-stuffed furniture and a dining table that will seat twelve or a compact sofa, lounge chairs and a table for two? Architects often help with the selection of furnishings, but you may want to hire an interior designer or select furnishings yourself. (See Chapter 9 for more information about furnishings.)

Preliminary Design is complete when you have made the major plan decisions (that is, the floor plan configuration, the basic dimensions of rooms and the three dimensional shape of the new spaces). Detailed decisions (the brand of refrigerator, the kind of light fixtures, the type of floor covering) will be made during the next phase.

Final Design or Construction Documents

During the final stage of design, the designer will prepare the drawings and specifications necessary to build your project and to obtain building permits from your community.

Making Decisions

You will continue to meet with your designer regularly during this phase. He or she will make recommendations about materials, finishes, fixtures and colors. Before you make decisions, ask about cost, availability and maintenance. (High cost items can take your project over budget; limited availability can delay your project; and difficult maintenance can be a nuisance in the future.) Ask to see samples, too. It makes the selection process easier and removes some of the mystery. Designers often have a range of sample materials and finishes, but they may send you to showrooms to see appliances, cabinets and fixtures. Although you can delay a few decisions until the construction phase, there is less potential for problems if you make decisions now. Your final decisions will appear in the plans and specifications.

A *Design Decision Checklist* and the following forms are included in this chapter for you to use in selecting finishes, fixtures and hardware:

✎ *Exterior Materials and Finishes.*
✎ *Room by Room Materials and Finishes.*
✎ *Appliances and Plumbing Fixtures.*

Again, do not be intimidated by the lists and forms. Your designer knows that all these decisions must be made; he or she can keep track of everything. These lists are intended to give you a complete picture so you can concentrate on what is important to you and leave the rest to others, if you want.

Final Plans

The final plans or construction drawings will show dimensions, materials and details, and locations of all light fixtures, switches, outlets, appliances and equipment. They will also indicate what is existing, what should be removed and what is new. Drawings may vary from a single sheet to many pages depending on the size and complexity of your project. Look at the example in this chapter. Final drawings may include:

- Site plan.
- Foundation plan.
- Floor plans (for each level of your project).
- Exterior elevations.
- Interior elevations.
- Roof plan.
- Framing plans.
- Heating, ventilating and plumbing plans.
- Electrical plans.
- Details.

Final plans also include specifications for materials. For a simple home remodeling, specifications may be written on the drawings. For a more complex project, a specification pamphlet or book may be prepared which lists all materials and describes requirements for construction and installation.

Making a Final Cost Estimate

When final drawings are almost complete, the designer may have a final cost estimate prepared. This estimate will be more accurate than the preliminary estimate because the plans are detailed and specific. But often a designer will forgo a final cost estimate and obtain bids from contractors instead. A contractor's bid is a firm price, not just an estimate. If the project cost is too high at this point, it is often more expedient to try to reduce costs directly with a contractor. (See the *Cost Cutting Checklist* in Chapter 7.)

Financing Update

During final design, it is a good idea to make a tentative selection of a lender. You sometimes can secure the best financing with a lender that you know: the lender who holds your existing mortgage, the bank which has your checking or savings accounts or a credit union you have used. The lender will want to know the amount you want to borrow (use the preliminary cost estimate or more recent information) and may want to see your plans. Some lenders require completed plans, specifications and a construction bid before they will make a final loan commitment. Others do not. Be sure to find out all the requirements for loan applications and to learn how much time it will take to process the application. (Refer back to Chapter 3 for the *Financing Checklist* and any information you collected.) ■

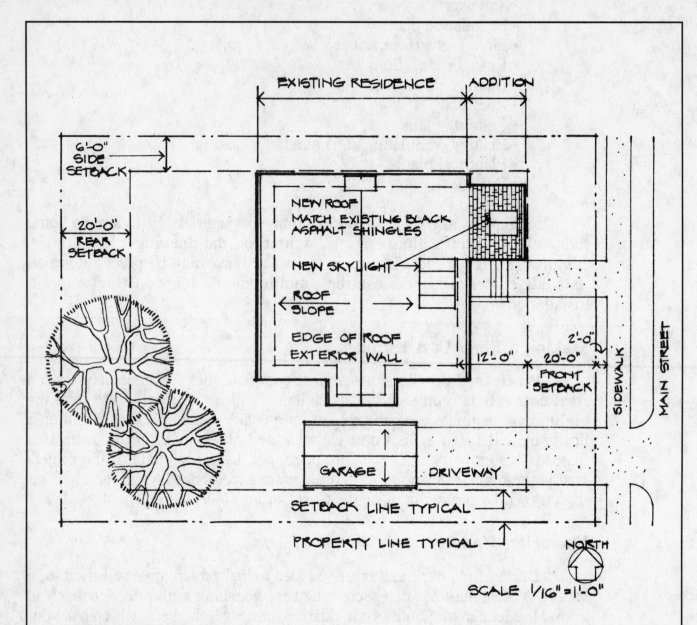

EXISTING RESIDENCE — ADDITION

6'-0" SIDE SETBACK

20'-0" REAR SETBACK

NEW ROOF MATCH EXISTING BLACK ASPHALT SHINGLES

NEW SKYLIGHT

ROOF SLOPE

EDGE OF ROOF EXTERIOR WALL

12'-0"

2'-0"

20'-0" FRONT SETBACK

SIDEWALK

MAIN STREET

GARAGE — DRIVEWAY

SETBACK LINE TYPICAL —

PROPERTY LINE TYPICAL —

NORTH

SCALE 1/16" = 1'-0"

SITE PLAN

SHOWS:
Property Lines
Building Setbacks
Location of House, Garage and Trees
Location of New Work/Addition
Walks and Driveway
Roof Plan (usually)
North Arrow and Scale of Drawing

Example of Final Drawings

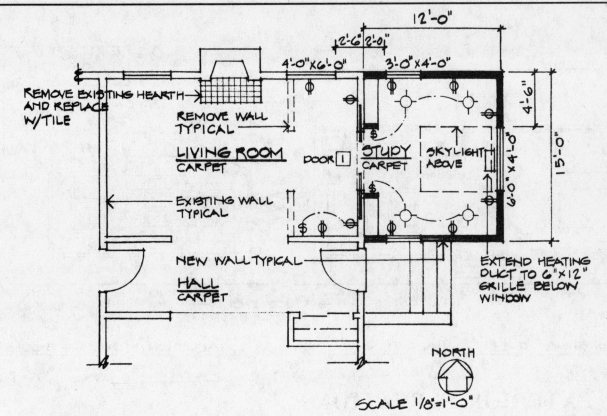

REMOVE EXISTING HEARTH AND REPLACE W/TILE

REMOVE WALL TYPICAL

LIVING ROOM
CARPET

DOOR 1

STUDY
CARPET

SKYLIGHT ABOVE

EXISTING WALL TYPICAL

NEW WALL TYPICAL

HALL
CARPET

EXTEND HEATING DUCT TO 6"×12" GRILLE BELOW WINDOW

12'-0"
2'-6" 2'-0"
4'-0"×6'-0"
3'-0"×4'-0"
4'-6"
6'-0"×4'-0"
15'-0"

NORTH

SCALE 1/8"=1'-0"

FLOOR PLAN

SHOWS:
Plan of Remodeled Area and/or Addition
Relationship to Existing House
Dimensions for Building New Work
Location and Size of Doors and Windows
Floor Materials

LEGEND
$ Switch
Ceiling Fixture
Convenience Outlet
(Electrical work may appear on
  this or a separate plan.)

FOUNDATION and FLOOR FRAMING PLAN

SHOWS:
Dimensions
Location, Size and Spacing of
   New Structural Work

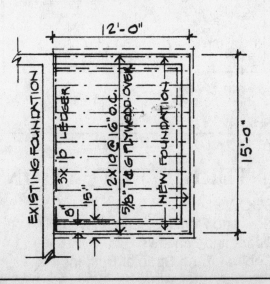

EXISTING FOUNDATION
3×10 LEDGER
2×10 @ 16" O.C.
5/8" T&G PLYWOOD OVER
NEW FOUNDATION
12'-0"
15'-0"
6"
15"

Example of Final Drawings

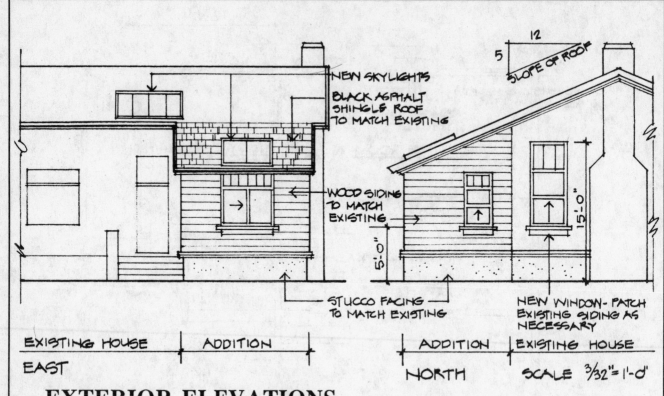

NEW SKYLIGHTS

BLACK ASPHALT SHINGLE ROOF TO MATCH EXISTING

12
5
SLOPE OF ROOF

WOOD SIDING TO MATCH EXISTING

15'-0"

5'-0"

STUCCO FACING TO MATCH EXISTING

NEW WINDOW - PATCH EXISTING SIDING AS NECESSARY

EXISTING HOUSE | ADDITION

EAST

ADDITION | EXISTING HOUSE

NORTH   SCALE 3/32"= 1'-0'

EXTERIOR ELEVATIONS

SHOWS:
Existing, Remodeled and New Exterior Walls
Doors and Windows

Materials, Heights of New Work
Slope of Roof

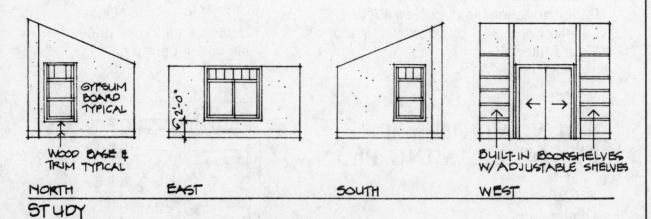

GYPSUM BOARD TYPICAL

WOOD BASE & TRIM TYPICAL

2'-0"

BUILT-IN BOOKSHELVES W/ ADJUSTABLE SHELVES

NORTH   EAST   SOUTH   WEST

STUDY

INTERIOR ELEVATIONS

SHOWS:
New and Remodeled Interior Walls
Doors and Windows
Cabinets and Special Built-ins

Materials
Heights of New Work

Example of Final Drawings

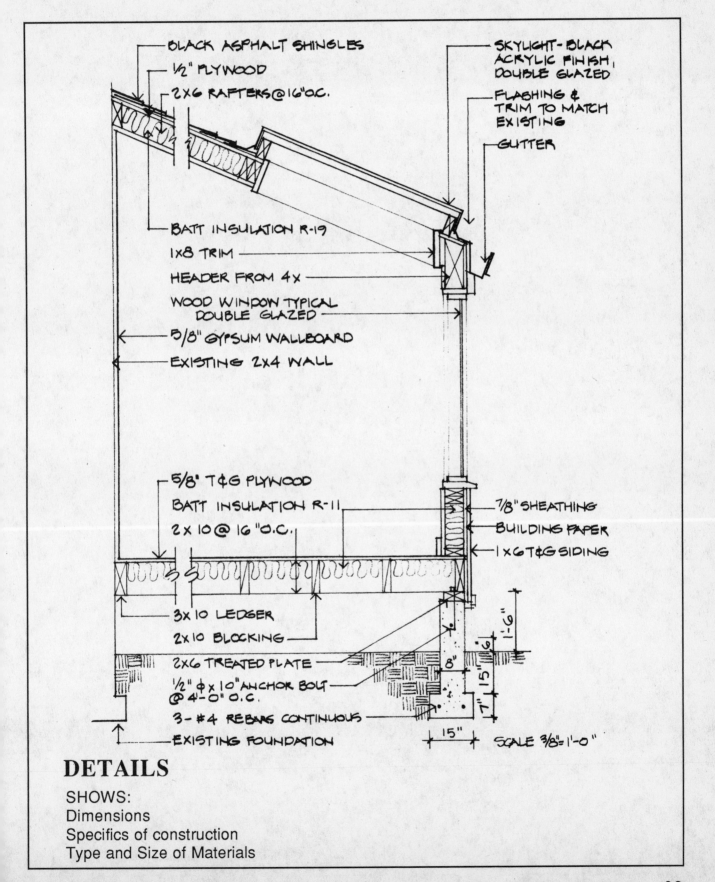

BLACK ASPHALT SHINGLES

½" PLYWOOD

2X6 RAFTERS @ 16"O.C.

SKYLIGHT-BLACK ACRYLIC FINISH, DOUBLE GLAZED

FLASHING & TRIM TO MATCH EXISTING

GUTTER

BATT INSULATION R-19

1x8 TRIM

HEADER FROM 4x

WOOD WINDOW TYPICAL DOUBLE GLAZED

5/8" GYPSUM WALLBOARD

EXISTING 2x4 WALL

5/8" T&G PLYWOOD

BATT INSULATION R-11

2 x 10 @ 16 "O.C.

7/8" SHEATHING

BUILDING PAPER

1 x 6 T&G SIDING

3x10 LEDGER

2x10 BLOCKING

2x6 TREATED PLATE

½" Ø x 10" ANCHOR BOLT @ 4-0" O.C.

3- #4 REBARS CONTINUOUS

EXISTING FOUNDATION

1'-6"

6"

15"

8"

7"

15"

SCALE 3/8"=1'-0"

DETAILS

SHOWS:
Dimensions
Specifics of construction
Type and Size of Materials

Design Tastes

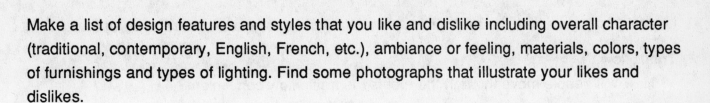

Make a list of design features and styles that you like and dislike including overall character (traditional, contemporary, English, French, etc.), ambiance or feeling, materials, colors, types of furnishings and types of lighting. Find some photographs that illustrate your likes and dislikes.

What I Like in Design:

1. _____
2. _____
3. _____
4. _____
5. _____
6. _____
7. _____
8. _____
9. _____
10. _____

What I Dislike in Design:

1. _____
2. _____
3. _____
4. _____
5. _____

Plan Review Checklist

Use this list to evaluate the preliminary plans that your designer or contractor prepares.

Traffic flow.
- How will people move through the rooms? Is traffic flow convenient?
- Is there enough room for comfortable traffic flow? (Are there congested areas?)
- Will furniture disrupt easy traffic flow?

Size and shape of rooms.
- Do the rooms have adequate space for the desired uses?
- Will the furniture you want fit in the room?

Use of the rooms.
- Is there enough privacy?
- Is there enough separation between noisy and quiet areas?
- Is storage/closet space adequate?
- Is there enough wall space to locate furniture (for example, is there wall space for beds in the bedrooms)?

Doors.
- Will doors swing into traffic flow or furniture? Will they create other problems?
- Are there appropriate locations near doors for light switches?
- Are there enough doors or too many doors?

Windows and skylights.
- Is there enough natural light?
- Can you (do you want to) control direct sunlight? If so, is there adequate space for stacks of draperies, opened shutters, blinds or shades?
- Is there enough ventilation?
- Do windows frame the views that you want to see?
- Are windows too big or too small?

Exterior.
- Do you think that the remodeled area will look appropriate with your existing home?

Miscellaneous
- How will the rooms be lighted?
- Are there appropriate locations for home electronics (TV, radios, stereo, computer)?

Preliminary Construction Cost Estimate

Date _____

Construction cost estimates are often calculated for major divisions of work (examples are concrete, carpentry, doors and windows, finishes, electrical, etc.); see the reverse side of this page. Obtain a copy of the preliminary cost estimate, review it and use this worksheet for your notes.

Breakdown of Construction Cost Estimate

Item	Cost
1. _____	$_____
2. _____	$_____
3. _____	$_____
4. _____	$_____
5. _____	$_____
6. _____	$_____
7. _____	$_____
8. _____	$_____
9. _____	$_____
10. _____	$_____
11. _____	$_____
12/14. _____	$_____
15. _____	$_____
16. _____	$_____

Total Estimated Cost $_____

Areas for Potential Cost Savings

Item	Cost
_____	$_____
_____	$_____
_____	$_____
_____	$_____
_____	$_____
_____	$_____

Total Estimated Savings $_____

TOTAL ADJUSTED ESTIMATED CONSTRUCTION COST $_____

Construction Cost Estimate Divisions

The following is a list of standard construction divisions often used by estimators to calculate estimated costs or by contractors to make a construction bid. The divisions are subtotaled and then the contractor's overhead and profit are added.

DIVISION	SUBDIVISION
1.0 Preliminary and General Conditions	.1 Permits, plan check, debris box .2 Final clean-up (allowance)
2.0 Site Work	.1 Demolition .2 Site preparation and excavation .3 Paving, patios and walks .4 Landscape planting and irrigation
3.0 Concrete	.1 Foundations, slabs and piers
4.0 Masonry	.1 Masonry walls, fireplace, hearth and facing
5.0 Metal	.1 Rough hardware .2 Finish hardware
6.0 Carpentry	.1 Rough lumber and labor .2 Finish lumber and labor (including siding) .3 Cabinets .4 Countertops
7.0 Thermal and Moisture Protection	.1 Insulation, weather stripping and thresholds .2 Roofing .3 Skylights
8.0 Doors and Windows	.1 Doors and garage door .2 Windows .3 Sliding glass doors .4 Hardware
9.0 Finishes	.1 Plaster or stucco .2 Gypsum wallboard .3 Resilient and wood flooring .4 Carpeting .5 Painting .6 Ceramic tile
10.0 Specialties	.1 Shower enclosure .2 Bathroom accessories
11.0 Equipment	.1 Appliances
12.0, 13.0, 14.0	(Not used)
15.0 Mechanical	.1 Plumbing .2 Heating, ventilation and air conditioning
16.0 Electrical	.1 Wiring and electrical fixtures

SUBTOTAL $ _____

Insurance
Contractor's overhead and profit (approx. 15%)

TOTAL ESTIMATED CONSTRUCTION COST $ _____

Design Decision Checklist

This list outlines materials, finishes, fixtures and hardware that you may select for your home remodeling project.

Exterior

☐ **Wall Material**
___ Match existing
___ Wood (siding, shingles, plywood)
___ Masonry (brick, stone adobe, concrete block)
___ Plaster or stucco
___ Metal siding

☐ **Roofing Material**
___ Match existing
___ Wood shakes or shingles
___ Composition or asphalt shingles
___ Tile
___ Slate
___ Built-up roofing (for flat roofs)

☐ **Trim**
___ Door and window trim
___ Roof fascia and trim

☐ **Doors**
___ Match existing
___ Wood, steel or aluminum
___ Flush, panel or frame with glass
___ Hinged or sliding

☐ **Windows**
___ Match existing
___ Wood, steel or aluminum
___ Sliding, casement, awning or double hung
___ Clear or tinted glass

☐ **Paving and/or Decks**
___ Concrete
___ Brick
___ Stone
___ Ceramic tile
___ Wood

Interior

☐ **Wall Material and Finish**
__ Wallboard with paint
(smooth or textured finish)
__ Wallboard with wallpaper
__ Plaster
__ Wood (paneling or plywood)
__ Masonry (brick, stone or
concrete block)
__ Ceramic tile

☐ **Flooring Material**
__ Wall to wall carpeting
__ Wood (planks, strips or parquet)
with or without area rugs
__ Ceramic tile
__ Vinyl (sheet or tiles)

☐ **Trim**
__ Baseboard
__ Door and window trim
__ Molding

☐ **Hardware**
__ Style and finish
__ Door knobs and locksets
__ Hinges
__ Cabinet pulls

☐ **Fireplace**
__ Type (built-in masonry, pre-built
metal or wood burning stove)
__ Facing and hearth (fire-proof)
__ Gas fire starter

☐ **Ceiling Material and Finish**
__ Wallboard with paint
__ Wallboard with wallpaper
__ Plaster
__ Wood (paneling or plywood)
__ Exposed beam
__ Acoustical tile

☐ **Electrical**
__ Light fixtures (recessed, ceiling
mounted, suspended, indirect
or lamps)
__ Switch plates (where and what color)
__ Electrical outlets (where, what color,
how high off the floor or counter)
__ Telephone
__ Television, cable
__ Electrical security system
__ Location of home electronics equip-
ment (TV's, VCR, stereo, radios,
personal computer)

☐ **Mechanical Systems** (Heating,
ventilation and air conditioning)
__ Heating (central forced-air furnace.
electric, radiant, active or
passive solar)
__ Ventilation (fans, open windows)
__ Air conditioning

Kitchen and Bathroom

KITCHEN

☐ **Cabinets**
  __ Material
    __ Wood (natural or painted)
    __ Plastic laminate
    __ Metal
  __ Style (contemporary, traditional, open, closed, etc.)
  __ Countertops
    __ Plastic laminate
    __ Ceramic tile
    __ Butcher block
    __ Stone
    __ Synthetic marble
    __ Stainless steel
  __ Hardware (pulls, hinges)
  __ Height of work surfaces
  __ Special storage (location of pantry, spices, trash, etc.)

☐ **Appliances**
  __ Electric or gas
  Major
    __ Refrigerator
    __ Range/cooktop and ovens
    __ Fan
    __ Microwave
    __ Dishwasher
    __ Disposal
    __ Trash compactor
    __ Washing machine
    __ Clothes dryer
  __ Location of small appliances (Coffee maker, food processor, toaster, toaster oven)
  __ Location of misc. appliances (Radio, television, stereo)

☐ **Plumbing fixtures**
  __ Sink
  __ Bar sink
  __ Laundry sink
  __ Hot water heater

☐ **Storage** (cookbooks, broom closet)

BATHROOM

☐ **Cabinets**
  __ Material
  __ Style   } see kitchen
  __ Countertop
  __ Hardware

☐ **Plumbing fixtures**
  __ Bathtub
  __ Shower
  __ Sink
  __ Toilet and toilet seat

☐ **Plumbing fittings**
  __ Shower head
  __ Bathtub faucet and handles
  __ Sink faucet and handles

☐ **Miscellaneous**
  __ Towel bars
  __ Hooks
  __ Toilet paper holder
  __ Medicine cabinet
  __ Soap and toothbrush holders
  __ Mirrors
  __ Fan
  __ Heater
  __ Sunlamp

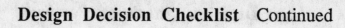

Furnishings

☐ **Chairs**
— Lounge chairs
— Dining chairs
— Kitchen chairs
— Bar stools
— Desk chairs
— Chaise lounge

☐ **Sofas**
— Sectional
— Standard sofa
— Loveseat
— Sofa bed

☐ **Tables**
— Dining table
— Kitchen table
— Coffee table
— End tables
— TV table
— VCR table
— Bedroom night stand
— Card table

☐ **Desks**
— Adults
— Children
— Computer

☐ **Beds**
— Adult (king, queen, full)
— Children (twin, bunk, trundel)
— Sofa bed
— Futon

☐ **Storage**
— Bookcases
— File cabinets
— Chest of drawers
— Armoire
— Credenza or buffet
— Stereo cabinet
— Other home electronics storage

☐ **Entertainment**
— TV
— Stereo and speakers
— Radios
— Piano
— VCR

☐ **Window Coverings**
— Draperies
— Shades
— Blinds (horizontal or vertical)
— Shutters

☐ **Accessories**
— Lamps
— Pictures
— Pillows
— Plants
— Vases
— Wastebaskets

Exterior Materials and Finishes

Outline your selection of exterior materials and finishes on this form.

BUILDING ITEM	MATERIAL	FINISH	COLOR
Walls	_____	_____	_____
Windows	_____	_____	_____
Doors	_____	_____	_____
Trim	_____	_____	_____
Paving/decks	_____	_____	_____
Roof	_____	_____	_____
Other	_____	_____	_____
	_____	_____	_____
	_____	_____	_____
	_____	_____	_____

ELECTRICAL	MANUFACTURER	NAME/NUMBER	FINISH
Light fixtures	1 _____	_____	_____
	2 _____	_____	_____
	3 _____	_____	_____
	4 _____	_____	_____
	5 _____	_____	_____

MISCELLANEOUS

Light fixture locations.

Electrical outlet locations.

Hose hook-up (hose bibb) locations.

Downspout and gutter locations.

Room by Room Materials and Finishes

ROOM _____

Outline your selection of interior materials and finishes. Use a separate form for each room.

BUILDING ITEM	MATERIAL	FINISH	COLOR
Floor	_____	_____	_____
Baseboard	_____	_____	_____
Walls	_____	_____	_____
Trim	_____	_____	_____
Ceiling	_____	_____	_____
Molding	_____	_____	_____
Cabinets	_____	_____	_____
Interiors	_____	_____	_____
Counter height	_____		
Countertop	_____	_____	_____
Other built-ins	_____	_____	_____
Other	_____	_____	_____
	_____	_____	_____
	_____	_____	_____

DOORS	TYPE	FINISH	HARDWARE
1	_____	_____	_____
2	_____	_____	_____
3	_____	_____	_____

ELECTRICAL	MANUFACTURER	NAME/NUMBER	FINISH
Light fixtures 1	_____	_____	_____
2	_____	_____	_____
3	_____	_____	_____
4	_____	_____	_____
5	_____	_____	_____

FURNISHINGS			
1	_____	_____	_____
2	_____	_____	_____
3	_____	_____	_____

MISCELLANEOUS   Electrical outlets, switch plates: Location, height above floor, color.

Room by Room Materials and Finishes

ROOM _____

Outline your selection of interior materials and finishes. Use a separate form for each room.

BUILDING ITEM	MATERIAL	FINISH	COLOR
Floor	_____	_____	_____
Baseboard	_____	_____	_____
Walls	_____	_____	_____
Trim	_____	_____	_____
Ceiling	_____	_____	_____
Molding	_____	_____	_____
Cabinets			
Interiors	_____	_____	_____
Counter height	_____		
Countertop	_____	_____	_____
Other built-ins	_____	_____	_____
Other	_____	_____	_____
	_____	_____	_____
	_____	_____	_____

DOORS	TYPE	FINISH	HARDWARE
1	_____	_____	_____
2	_____	_____	_____
3	_____	_____	_____

ELECTRICAL	MANUFACTURER	NAME/NUMBER	FINISH
Light fixtures 1	_____	_____	_____
2	_____	_____	_____
3	_____	_____	_____
4	_____	_____	_____
5	_____	_____	_____

FURNISHINGS			
1	_____	_____	_____
2	_____	_____	_____
3	_____	_____	_____

MISCELLANEOUS   Electrical outlets, switch plates: Location, height above floor, color.

Room by Room Materials and Finishes

ROOM _____

Outline your selection of interior materials and finishes. Use a separate form for each room.

BUILDING ITEM	MATERIAL	FINISH	COLOR
Floor	_____	_____	_____
Baseboard	_____	_____	_____
Walls	_____	_____	_____
Trim	_____	_____	_____
Ceiling	_____	_____	_____
Molding	_____	_____	_____
Cabinets	_____	_____	_____
Interiors	_____	_____	_____
Counter height	_____		
Countertop	_____	_____	_____
Other built-ins	_____	_____	_____
Other	_____	_____	_____
	_____	_____	_____
	_____	_____	_____

DOORS	TYPE	FINISH	HARDWARE
1	_____	_____	_____
2	_____	_____	_____
3	_____	_____	_____

ELECTRICAL	MANUFACTURER	NAME/NUMBER	FINISH
Light fixtures 1	_____	_____	_____
2	_____	_____	_____
3	_____	_____	_____
4	_____	_____	_____
5	_____	_____	_____

FURNISHINGS			
1	_____	_____	_____
2	_____	_____	_____
3	_____	_____	_____

MISCELLANEOUS   Electrical outlets, switch plates: Location, height above floor, color.

Appliances and Plumbing Fixtures

Outline your selection of appliances and plumbing fixtures.

APPLIANCES	MANUFACTURER	NAME/NUMBER	COLOR
Refrigerator			
Range or Cooktop			
Fan/Hood			
Ovens			
Microwave			
Dishwasher			
Disposal			
Trash Compactor			
Washing Machine			
Clothes Dryer			

PLUMBING FIXTURES

Kitchen Sink			
Faucet Set			
Bar Sink			
Faucet Set			
Laundry Sink			
Faucet Set			
Bathroom Sink			
Faucet Set			
Toilet			
Toilet Seat			
Bathtub			
Faucet Set			
Shower			
Faucet Set			

MISCELLANEOUS HARDWARE

Towel Bars			
Hooks			
Toilet Paper Holder			
Medicine Cabinet			
Soap Dish			
Toothbrush Holder			

Design Meeting Memo

Date _____

Attending:

Name	Representing
_____	_____
_____	_____
_____	_____
_____	_____

Items Covered:

1. _____
   _____
2. _____
   _____
3. _____
   _____
4. _____
   _____
5. _____
   _____
6. _____
   _____

Action for Next Meeting:	**Person Responsible:**	**Date for Answer**
1. _____	_____	_____
_____		
2. _____	_____	_____
_____		
3. _____	_____	_____
_____		
4. _____	_____	_____
_____		
5. _____	_____	_____
_____		
6. _____	_____	_____
_____		

Design Meeting Memo

Date _____

Attending:

Name   Representing

_____   _____

_____   _____

_____   _____

_____   _____

Items Covered:

1. _____

_____

2. _____

_____

3. _____

_____

4. _____

_____

5. _____

_____

6. _____

_____

	Person Responsible:	**Date for Answer**
Action for Next Meeting:		
1. _____	_____	_____
2. _____	_____	_____
3. _____	_____	_____
4. _____	_____	_____
5. _____	_____	_____
6. _____	_____	_____

Design Meeting Memo

Date _____

Attending:

Name	Representing
_____	_____
_____	_____
_____	_____
_____	_____

Items Covered:

1. _____

2. _____

3. _____

4. _____

5. _____

6. _____

Action for Next Meeting: **Person Responsible:**   **Date for Answer**

1. _____ _____ _____

2. _____ _____ _____

3. _____ _____ _____

4. _____ _____ _____

5. _____ _____ _____

6. _____ _____ _____

7

ACTION.

WORKSHEETS.

POTENTIAL PROBLEMS AND PITFALLS.

☛ SELECT A RELIABLE CONTRACTOR WHO HAS A GOOD PERFORMANCE RECORD. A good contractor is EXTREMELY important.

☛ BEFORE THE CONTRACTOR BEGINS CONSTRUCTION, SIGN A CONTRACT THAT CLEARLY STATES YOUR MUTUAL AGREEMENT. A good contract helps prevent problems.

Bidding and Contractor Selection

After the final plans are complete, the next step is to obtain bids from contractors and select a specific contractor to build your project. A good contractor is EXTREMELY important. Make certain that any contractor you hire has sufficient experience and good recommendations. Construction is a difficult part of remodeling and it is critical to select a responsible and reliable contractor. He or she will manage construction effectively and efficiently and will have experience solving problems in a cooperative manner.

Most states license contractors as a consumer protection measure since construction work involves life safety and large sums of money. The state of California, for example, requires that a licensed contractor perform any work that will cost more than $200.00 for labor and materials together. ALWAYS choose a licensed contractor. Since the contractor will be working in your home every day for the duration of construction, it is important to select someone that you think you can "live with", as well.

Decide How You Will Contract for Your Project

Before you obtain bids on your project, you must decide what type of contractor you need and whether you will bid or negotiate the contract price. Your designer can help you decide.

Types of Contractors

There are two basic categories of contractors:

General contractor.

A general contractor is a professional builder who is responsible for construction of a project from beginning to end. General contractors typically employ their own workers to do carpentry and miscellaneous labor, but they hire specialized subcontractors for each separate remodeling project to perform electrical work, plumbing, painting and other trades. General contractors must pass a specific "general contractors' exam" to earn a license from the state.

A general contractor's responsibilities include:

- Providing all labor and construction materials needed to complete the project. The contractor and subcontractors perform the work and purchase all materials. If you can purchase some of the materials at a savings, inform the contractor. Many are willing to build with owner-supplied materials if they can plan in advance.
- Hiring and paying all specialized subcontractors and material suppliers.
- Managing and coordinating the construction work.
  (He or she schedules the workmen and subcontractors to be there at the right time and makes certain that the work gets done.)
- Managing the overall construction schedule.
- Coordinating with the owner and/or designer to solve problems, answer questions and make changes.
- Obtaining building permits.
- Arranging for required city/county building inspections.
- Handling workers' compensation insurance, state and federal tax forms and other state requirements for employers.
- Maintaining safe working conditions on the job site.

Subcontractor.

A subcontractor is a specialized builder who performs only one trade or one area of construction like roofing, electrical work, cabinet making or painting. Subcontractors, too, must be licensed by the state in their specialties. If your project involves just two or three specific tasks, such as installing a new roof, painting the exterior of your house or installing new kitchen cabinets, you may want to hire specialized subcontractors directly to do the work. If there are three or more different types of work involved in your project, it is a good idea to hire a general contractor. If you are considering being your own general contractor, review *Ways to Save Money* in Chapter 3.

A subcontractor's responsibilities include:

- Providing all labor and construction materials necessary for completion of his work.
- Obtaining necessary permits.
- Arranging for required city/county building inspections.

Bidding versus Negotiation

Bidding and negotiation are the two primary ways to obtain prices from contractors for construction work and bidding is more common. A bid is an offer to perform work for a specified price. In order to get competitive bids for comparison, give copies of the plans and specifications for your project to two, three or four contractors. It is important that you give the same information to each contractor so that each bid will be based on performing exactly the same work. The contractors will prepare written bid proposals and submit them to you within the time that you specify, usually two to four weeks.

A second way to hire a contractor is to negotiate the contract price. Negotiation involves selecting a contractor first, then agreeing upon the specific work to be done and the price. The advantage of negotiating is that you <u>may</u> be able to save money by designing with the contractor's participation. If you select a contractor early in the design process, you and your designer can work with him from the beginning to select the most cost effective systems. In addition, plans may require less detail for the contractor who has helped design the building systems. Opinions differ; many people believe that you receive better prices if more than one contractor bids on the project.

Contractors and Bonding

You may have heard references to "contractors and bonding" and wondered whether it applies to you. There are two basic types of bonds associated with home remodeling contractors.

• License bond.
Many states require that each licensed contractor posts a bond with the state licensing board before the state will grant a license. This bond does not guarantee that your job will be completed.

• Performance bond, and labor and materials bond.
These two bonds together assure the owner that the project will be completed as per contract. If the contractor defaults, the surety bonding organization will provide for completion of the project. The owner is protected up to the amount of the bonds, usually written for the total contract amount.

Most contractors can obtain these bonds at your request. Performance and labor and materials bonds are written for each specific job; a contractor does not have long-term bonding coverage. Some competent contractors are unable to obtain these bonds because their companies are too small. The owner pays for the bonds, usually one to five percent of the contract amount, so you must decide if you want them. The bonds are often requested to be part of the contractor's bid.

Finding Contractors

Finding a contractor is similar to finding a design consultant. Collect a list of contractors' names using the *Names of Contractors* form. Sources are:

- Friends and business acquaintances.
- Your architect or designer.
- The real estate section of local newspapers or magazines.
- Remodeling projects that you see under construction.
- Local contractors' associations.
- Material suppliers.
- The Yellow Pages of your phone directory.
  (Again, this is not your best source. But contractors do advertise, so you probably will be able to tell if residential work is a contractor's specialty.)

Telephone the list of contractors, describe your project and ask the following:

- Is the contractor interested in building your project?
- Does the contractor normally build projects like yours? (Ask the contractor to describe similar work.)
- Is the contractor licensed?
- How long has the contractor been in business?
- Can the contractor start construction when you want?

Arrange interviews with the interested contractors and discuss your project further. (The contractors may want to visit your home to see the project area.) Ask questions from the *Contractor Selection* worksheet in this chapter. Obtain both client and business references and request permission to call them. Also arrange to see some of the contractors' completed remodeling projects.

Then contact the references. Good recommendations are VERY important in contractor selection.

- Talk to the contractors' former clients. Satisfied clients are a good indication that the contractor will perform well for you. Use the *Questions for Contractors' Clients* worksheet.
- Contact bank and credit references, material suppliers and subcontractors to verify that the contractors pay their bills. This is a standard practice.
- Call the local office of the Contractors' State Licensing agency and ask if the contractors have licenses in good standing.
- Check with your local Better Business Bureau to see if any complaints have been registered about a contractor. (The California Better Business Bureau states that remodeling and home-improvement businesses receive the second highest number of complaints, after phone and mail order sales.)
- Verify contractors' insurance coverage with their carriers.

Bidding Your Project

Select two or three good contractors to bid on your project. You or your designer will give them each copies of your plans and specifications for bidding. The contractors will submit written bids to you within the time that you specify, usually two to four weeks. Like cost estimates, bids should be broken down into subdivisions of work with associated costs: there should be detail, not just a grand total. Contractor's overhead and profit will be added as the final element of the bid. Refer back to the *Construction Cost Estimate Divisions* worksheet in Chapter 6.

If you have chosen to negotiate your project, your selected contractor will prepare a total bid amount based on the final plans and specifications that he or she helped to develop.

Selecting a Contractor

You and your designer should review the bids AND all the information about the contractors. (Remember that good recommendations are very important.) Make certain that everything you want is included in the written bid. Then select the contractor that you believe will build the best project. Base your final selection on the following:

Performance and reliability.
SELECT A RELIABLE CONTRACTOR WITH A GOOD PERFORMANCE RECORD.

Experience.
Select a contractor who has experience. (It is not a good decision to let a "nice guy" learn about contracting at your expense.) Also it is wise to match your project with a contractor who builds projects of the same type and size. For example, if your remodeling is small, it will receive more attention and understanding from a contractor who typically builds small projects than one who always works with larger remodelings.

Communication and responsiveness.
As with your designer, be sure that you can communicate easily with your contractor. There always will be some problems to solve and you probably will want to make changes. It is important to select a contractor who will be responsive.

Bid price.
Of course, bid price is an important factor. Owners frequently select the lowest bidder, but you are not required to do so. In fact, beware of any bid which is substantially below the others. Just remember to evaluate all the above factors when you make a final selection.

Reducing Costs

Sometimes the lowest bid on a project will be significantly higher than estimated and more than you wanted to spend. If this happens, you must decide if you want to build the more costly project, build the project after making changes to reduce cost or not build at all. Any of these changes is a difficult decision.

If you decide to try to reduce costs, meet with your designer and the contractor that you prefer and review his or her bid. Ask the contractor to suggest ways to reduce costs. You may be able to substitute less expensive materials, eliminate unnecessary elements from the project, do some of the work yourself or redesign a smaller/simpler project. Examine the *Cost Cutting Checklist* in this chapter.

The Contract Between You and Your Contractor

BEFORE THE CONTRACTOR BEGINS ANY WORK, PREPARE AND SIGN A CONTRACT THAT CLEARLY STATES YOUR MUTUAL AGREEMENT. A good contract is one of the best means of assuring that you will get what you want. As stated before, a good contract helps prevent problems. Remember that it is binding for both of you. The contractor may provide a contract form; you can purchase standard contract forms from the American Institute of Architects; or your legal counsel can prepare one.

Your contract should cover the following items. Use the *Construction Contract Checklist* at the end of this chapter when you prepare your contract.

Materials and work included.
Briefly describe the construction work to be done. Also include a list of materials and equipment that will be used and installed. Usually the plans and specifications serve this purpose and are made part of the contract by reference. It will prevent misunderstandings about what the contractor's price includes. Also cover the following:

- Describe demolition work and state who will be responsible for removal of debris.
- Designate who will obtain permits, pay fees and arrange for inspections.
- If you or other contractors will do some of the work, describe it and how the work will be coordinated with the general contractor's work.
- Designate the boundaries of construction activity and areas you want to keep free from dust and debris. (Construction is not a clean or delicate job.)
- State whether or not you want the job site to be cleaned up each night.
- Designate the locations where the contractor may bring heavy equipment onto the site and where he can store building materials when they are delivered.

Warranties.
The contractor should provide a warranty for his work. The warranty often extends for a year from the completion date. Find out what is customary in your community. Describe the conditions of the warranty in your contract. The contractor also should provide quarantees and warranties for appliances, equipment and materials as appropriate.

Time schedule.

Stipulate the construction starting and completion dates in the contract after confirming the amount of time the contractor will require. (It is usually best to plan construction when the weather will be good and when it will be most convenient for your family, often summertime).

The completion date is usually a target rather than a guarantee. There are often unforeseen delays, such as slow material shipments, bad weather or scheduling conflicts that prolong construction. If it is very important that your project be completed by a specific date, you might consider offering the contractor an incentive payment if he finishes early or even if he finishes on time.

Although they are rarely used in residential contracts and difficult to enforce, "liquidated damages" are another way to emphasize the time schedule. The owner must prove that a time delay will result in direct financial loss. Liquidated damages are per day payments (related to the amount of the per day loss) made by the contractor to the owner from the time a project was supposed to be finished until the actual date of completion. If you consider liquidated damages, consult your attorney.

Payment.

State the agreed upon price and list a schedule of payments. Contractors are typically paid in monthly installments based on the percent of total work they have completed (including delivery of construction materials to the site.) If the project will take a short amount of time, the contractor may request weekly or bi-weekly installments.

Retention or withholding.

It is a common practice to withhold 10% of each payment to the contractor, called retention or withholding. The final 10% of the total contract amount is paid 30 to 60 days after substantial completion of the project and after the lien period has expired. (See the next section on liens.) DO NOT MAKE YOUR FINAL PAYMENT TO THE CONTRACTOR UNTIL YOU ARE SATISFIED THAT ALL THE WORK IS COMPLETE.

Liens and lien releases.

A lien is a legal claim placed by one person on the property of another to obtain payment for a debt or obligation. Lien laws vary from state to state but in general, any person (contractor or subcontractor) who has provided labor or materials for your home remodeling and has filed the required "preliminary lien notice" is entitled to file a lien against your property if he or she does not receive payment. Liens are filed with the court.

When your project begins, you may receive "preliminary lien notices" in the mail. Do not be alarmed; these are simply notices informing you that various parties are working on your job and establishing their rights to file a lien if necessary. Many subcontractors do this as standard practice.

However, if the general contractor fails to pay a subcontractor, he or she may file a "Claim of Lien" or "Mechanics Lien" against your property. If someone files a lien, you may have to pay him directly. The court may require you to pay the party filing the lien even if you have paid the general contractor in full. In most states, a lien must be filed within the 30 to 60 day "lien period" after the job is finished. Verify the length of the lien period in your state. If a lien is filed against your property at any time, consult your legal counsel.

Your contract should state that the contractor must submit to you evidence of release of liens. Lien releases prevent workers from filing liens on your property in the future. They are prepared after all construction is complete. Since lien laws vary from state to state, there is no single format for release of liens. One alternative is that the contractor will obtain and give you copies of separate lien release forms signed by each subcontractor or material supplier who worked on your project stating that the general contractor has paid him or her in full. Another alternative is that the contractor will submit the AIA document "Contractor's Affidavit of Payment of Debts and Claims", a sworn statement declaring that all the workers have been paid. Find out what is acceptable in your state.

Miscellaneous.
It is a good idea to include an arbitration clause and a statement about termination of agreement in case major disputes arise.

Review the contract thoroughly and consult your legal counsel before signing it. If you become uncomfortable with the contract after signing, you may be able to cancel. In some states homeowners have the right to cancel a contract within 3 days of signing it without penalty (contractors sometimes require a cancellation penalty of up to 25% of contract price after 3 days.) If you cancel, you should both call the contractor and send a written cancellation by registered mail. If you can work out your differences, sign a new contract. If not, look for a new contractor.

If you hire a general contractor, do not make separate agreements with subcontractors or workers without first consulting the general contractor. The general contractor is responsible for the entire project and all work should be coordinated with him. ∎

Names of Contractors

NAME and FIRM	PHONE	SOURCE	COMMENT
1 _____	_____	_____	_____
_____			_____
2 _____	_____	_____	_____
_____			_____
3 _____	_____	_____	_____
_____			_____
4 _____	_____	_____	_____
_____			_____
5 _____	_____	_____	_____
_____			_____
6 _____	_____	_____	_____
_____			_____
7 _____	_____	_____	_____
_____			_____
8 _____	_____	_____	_____
_____			_____

QUESTIONS TO ASK CONTRACTORS

Call the contractors on your list, describe your project including your budget and ask the following questions.

1. Are you interested in building my project?
2. Have you built projects like this before and do you currently work on projects like this? (the same size and type)
3. Describe some of your work/similar projects.
4. How long have you been in business?
   Are you licensed?
5. I would like to start building in _____ (what month); will my project fit into your work schedule?

Notes

Contractor Selection

Date _____

Firm _____ Representative _____

Address _____ Phone No. _____

_____ Recommended by _____

My Project is: _____ My Budget is: $ _____

Experience:

How many similar projects have you built? _____

Examples _____

_____

How long in business? _____ How many employees ? _____

What is your contractors' license number? _____

Have you worked in my community before? Yes _____ No _____

Do you have insurance coverage?

Workers' Compensation? Yes _____ No _____

Liability Insurance? Yes _____ No _____

Property Damage? Yes _____ No _____

When can you begin? _____ How long will construction take? _____

References:

Contractors' State License Board Comments. _____

_____

Better Business Bureau comments. _____

Client _____ Client _____

Address _____ Address _____

_____ _____

Phone _____ Phone _____

Comments _____ Comments _____

_____ _____

Bank _____ Supplier _____

Address _____ Address _____

_____ _____

Phone _____ Phone _____

Comments _____ Comments _____

_____ _____

My Evaluation:

Experience. _____

Performance. _____

Communication and Responsiveness _____

Capacity and Capability. _____

Questions for Contractors' Clients

1. Were you satisfied with the work of this contractor?

2. Was the contractor easy to work with on a day-to-day basis?

3. Was there any confusion about what was included in the contract price?

4. Was it easy to make changes along the way?

5. Were there any problems?

6. Did the workers arrive at the job when the contractor said they would?

7. Did the workers clean up around the work area regularly?

8. Were there any problems getting the contractor to finish the final details at the end of the job?
   Did the contractor finish the project on time?

9. WOULD YOU HIRE THE CONTRACTOR AGAIN?

Contractor Selection

Date _____

Firm _____   Representative _____
Address _____   Phone No. _____
_____   Recommended by _____
My Project is: _____   My Budget is: $ _____

Experience:

How many similar projects have you built? _____

    Examples _____
_____

How long in business? _____   How many employees ? _____

What is your contractors' license number? _____

Have you worked in my community before?   Yes _____   No _____

Do you have insurance coverage?

    Workers' Compensation?   Yes _____   No _____

    Liability Insurance?   Yes _____   No _____

    Property Damage?   Yes _____   No _____

When can you begin? _____   How long will construction take? _____

References:

Contractors' State License Board Comments. _____
_____

Better Business Bureau comments. _____

Client _____   Client _____
Address _____   Address _____
_____   _____

Phone _____   Phone _____
Comments _____   Comments _____
_____   _____

Bank _____   Supplier _____
Address _____   Address _____
_____   _____

Phone _____   Phone _____
Comments _____   Comments _____
_____   _____

My Evaluation:

Experience. _____
Performance. _____
Communication and Responsiveness _____
Capacity and Capability. _____

Questions for Contractors' Clients

1. Were you satisfied with the work of this contractor?

2. Was the contractor easy to work with on a day-to-day basis?

3. Was there any confusion about what was included in the contract price?

4. Was it easy to make changes along the way?

5. Were there any problems?

6. Did the workers arrive at the job when the contractor said they would?

7. Did the workers clean up around the work area regularly?

8. Were there any problems getting the contractor to finish the final details at the end of the job?
   Did the contractor finish the project on time?

9. WOULD YOU HIRE THE CONTRACTOR AGAIN?

Cost Cutting Checklist

If the contractors' bids are too high, you may be able to reduce construction cost by doing one or more of the following.

- **Change to less expensive materials.**
  - Doors.
  - Windows.
  - Exterior Wall Finish.
  - Roofing Material.
  - Floor Coverings.
  - Interior Wall and Ceiling Finishes.
  - Wall Covering.
  - Light fixtures.
  - Appliances.
  - Plumbing Fixtures.
  - Hardware.
  - Style and Finish of Cabinets.
  - Countertops.
  - Heating System.

- **Eliminate elements that are not absolutely necessary.**
  (You may be able to add them later.)
  - Eliminate/reduce the quantity of cabinets or built-ins.
  - Eliminate a fireplace.
  - Eliminate a wet bar.
  - Eliminate/reduce the size of skylights.

- **Do some work yourself.**
  - Do demolition work.
  - Install insulation.
  - Do painting.
  - Take care of daily clean-up.

- **Change the plans.**
  - Eliminate a room.
  - Simplify the plans.
  - Reduce the size of room/s.
  - Reduce ceiling heights.

Note: If you make significant changes in your plans, the designer may want additional fees to change the drawings. Be sure to ask.

Contract Between Owner and Contractor
Checklist

The following are some of the items that should appear in your contract with a contractor.

- **Owner and project name and address.**
- **Contractor name, address and license number.**
- **Description of work to be done.**
    - Demolition.
    - Construction.
    - Clean-up.
- **Materials and equipment.**
    - Include plans and specifications by reference in the contract.
      (Materials are usually listed in specifications; if not, include a list of materials.)
    - Designate area where construction will take place.
    - Define where heavy equipment may come onto your property.
    - Designate area where contractor may store construction materials.
- **Total contract price.**
- **Schedule of payments by owner to contractor.**
- **Percentage payment retention until all work is complete.**
- **Construction start and completion dates.**
- **Designation of party responsible for obtaining permits and arranging for inspections.**
- **Liens.**
    - Statement about owner's rights under the law. (Check your local laws.)
    - Lien release form requirements.
- **Description of non-contract work (work to be done by owner and/or others hired directly by the owner).**
- **Description of the Change Order Process.** (See "Making Changes" in Chapter 8.)
- **Arbitration clause.**
- **Termination of agreement clause.**
- **Definition of warranty period.**

Other possible contract items:
Liquidated damages.

Note: Before you sign any contract, it is wise to consult your legal counsel.

8

ACTION.

WORKSHEETS.

POTENTIAL PROBLEMS AND PITFALLS.

☛Keep track of the schedule closely. Construction often takes more time than anticipated: the building permit process may be slow; ordered materials may not arrive on time; bad weather may delay construction; or the contractor may be slow.

☛Keep track of construction. If problems occur, try to solve them promptly.

☛Unexpected existing conditions may cause changes in cost and schedule.

☛Make all changes in writing. Do not make assumptions.

The Construction Process

The construction process is perhaps the most difficult part of a home remodeling project. No matter how well you plan ahead, there are always some unknowns and there may be changes and problems during construction. It is disruptive when a portion of your home is torn apart, and it is very stressful to live in the midst of on-going construction or to confuse your daily routines by moving out of your home. You will probably experience second thoughts when demolition begins. You may not understand much about construction and you may find it odd that workers are there all day sometimes and other times they appear only for a short time. Furthermore, no one told you that it might be THIS bad (wallboard dust will permeate every room; the water may be turned off for what seems like a month; it may rain after your roof is removed). Finally, it always seems to take twice as long as you ever imagined.

The Construction Process diagram in this chapter is a flowchart that shows a typical progression through construction. Review it as you read the following pages. The most important things you can do to help maintain some control and objectivity during construction include:

- Keep track of construction progress.
  (Know the planned time schedule, know what should happen each day and stay informed about changes in progress.)

- Do not be afraid to ask questions, especially if something does not look correct to you.

- Understand that there will be problems and changes.
  (Be flexible and try to make decisions in a timely manner.)

- Remember that construction is not a high-tech process.

Before Construction Begins

Before the contractor starts work, be sure to complete the required paperwork, have a preconstruction meeting with the designer and the contractor and make final plans for managing your household during construction. You can use the *Preconstruction Checklist* for reference.

Completing Paperwork

Required paperwork includes:

Financing.
Make final arrangements to borrow all the money that you will need for your project BEFORE the contractor begins any work, especially demolition. Loan approval often involves an appraisal of your existing residence. If walls are missing or kitchen cabinets have been removed, your home appraisal will be much less favorable. Sign all the documents and establish the terms of loan distribution. Some construction loans provide that payments be made directly to the general contractor.

Insurance.
Before construction begins, you should increase the insurance on your residence to cover the total cost of the completed remodeling or addition. Your new insurance coverage should include the replacement cost of both your existing home and the remodeling when it is complete. If something happens during construction, you could lose a large investment. It is your responsibility as the owner to insure the new work. Coverage should commence on the day that construction begins.

Construction contract.
The construction contract has been discussed in detail in Chapter 7. Make certain that both the contractor and you have a signed copy of the contract.

Building permit.
The contractor typically obtains the building permit (and subpermits, if necessary) from the city or county just before he or she is ready to start construction. Review Chapter 4. The designer or contractor will verify what submittals are required for the permit application. You may need to provide some information.

Typically a community requires these submittals:

- Plans and specifications. (More than one copy.)
- Address and description of property including lot and block number or assessor's parcel number.
- Value of proposed construction.
- Plan check and/or building permit fee. (Usually a percentage of construction cost.)
- Owner information. (Name and address.)
- Designer information. (Name and address.)
- Contractor information. (Name, address, license number, workers' compensation information.)
- Structural calculations. (Depends on the project.)
- Energy calculations. (Depends on the project.)

If you know that the permit process will take a long time (some communities need as long as two months), you may want to expedite the process by filing the permit application yourself before you have selected a contractor. In most communities, the contractor can provide his portion of the permit information when he secures the building permit from the issuing agency.

The Preconstruction Meeting with the Contractor

The designer usually arranges a preconstruction meeting to review the project and procedures before construction begins. (You should have a written contract with the designer about work that he or she will perform during construction.) If you are not working with a designer, arrange the meeting yourself. It is important to discuss the following:

Communication with the contractor.

Determine who will be the contractor's representative or job foreman. This person will be your primary contact during construction. You and/or your designer should address questions (and answers to questions) to this ONE individual. It will simplify communication and help prevent confusion. Contractors generally prefer that you do not give orders directly to the subcontractors and workers. Also inform the contractor to direct his questions to you (the project manager) or the designer (if appropriate).

Learn how you can contact the contractor in case of emergency (for example, the roof has been removed and it starts to rain in the middle of the night). Also inform the contractor how to contact you.

Plan for a regularly scheduled job meeting among owner, designer and contractor to review progress and discuss questions. Job meetings typically occur once a week but more often may be appropriate if the job will be short.

Ask the contractor to tell you what decisions remain and when you must make them.

Review the project details.
- The proposed work schedule. Ask the contractor to describe what is likely to happen during construction. (For example: the roofing will be removed during the fourth week and will be replaced within approximately 5 days; utility services will be turned off for two day intervals while plumbing and wiring are changed, and so on.) Some contractors will provide a written schedule.
- The contractor's working hours.
- Where the contractor should bring materials and equipment onto the site.
- Where the contractor should store materials and equipment on the site.
- The limits of construction work (what the workmen should avoid).
- Daily clean-up requirements.
- Home security requirements during construction.
- Procedure for making changes. (See the section on making changes in this chapter.)
- Submittal of contractor's invoices (where, when, what format).

Make Final Plans for the Household

THE CONSTRUCTION PHASE WILL BE STRESSFUL ON YOU AND YOUR FAMILY. Whether you move out or stay in your home, construction will upset your routines and environment. You will feel as if you are camping out and there is nowhere to retreat. Making preparations ahead of time will help minimize stress.

Prepare your home.
Move your family and your belongings out of the way or out of the house and be prepared for inconveniences. Necessary tasks may include:

- Arrange to live elsewhere or use rooms that are not being remodeled.

- Move all furniture, carpets and precious items away from the vicinity of construction.
- Cover or pack everything that you want to remain clean. Construction dust and dirt will expand to other rooms. (Make certain that you can find what you will need during construction.)
- Cover wall to wall carpeting will plastic sheets or drop cloths. (Construction workers are just doing their jobs and they may be unaware that they are tracking mud on your favorite carpet.)
- Remove tools, ladders and other items that you do not want construction workers to use. (They may be damaged during construction.)
- Plan how and where you will eat meals if your kitchen or eating area will be remodeled.
- Arrange to share neighbors' bathroom facilities if yours will be unusable for a few days.

Prepare your family.
By this time the family will be well aware of the impending changes. Describe the schedule, the arrangements and what will happen during construction. If you would like, prepare a schedule/calendar to hang on the wall. Update the schedule and talk with the family about progress regularly. Remember to make emotional allowances for family members as construction proceeds. (It is difficult for everyone, including the kids.)

Assign responsibilities to family members (assist with cleanup, water the plants, feed the dog) and write them down on the schedule.

Prepare yourself.
Make certain that your accumulated remodeling paperwork is together (plans and specifications, contracts, product information and correspondence) and that you are prepared to keep track of any new paperwork (bills and invoices, canceled checks, meeting memos, changes, preliminary lien notices, lien releases.) You may also want a place to keep material and color samples.

Plan diversions.
It is helpful to plan ahead for outside activities during construction to offset the disrupted home environment. Make a list of possible diversions and carry them out as appropriate throughout the project. Examples are:

- Have a construction progress party (or two). Show your friends and neighbors what is happening. You might have this event after the rough wall framing is in place and/or after the wallboard has been installed. Then everyone can see the shape of the new rooms. Have a simple party - beer and peanuts or wine and cheese.
- Go out to dinner more often - anything from fast food to your favorite special restaurant.
- Have simple picnic meals in the backyard.
- Go to movies.
- Go to parks and museums.
- Leave town for a weekend.
- Tell your friends about the remodeling. They may ask you to dinner or offer some help. (Or ask yourself to dinner.)

Keep your spirits up!
It will be worth it when construction is done. But your spirits are likely to take a roller coaster ride during the construction process:

- You will be excited before construction begins.
- You may have second thoughts after demolition is started and you are surrounded by mess.
- You will feel delighted after the rough framing is complete and you can see and stand in your new rooms.
- You may be frustrated and annoyed while the contractor is finishing the job. (It seems like it takes forever and the noise and dirt become less tolerable every day.)
- When the project nears completion, your spirits again will climb.

During Construction

The construction process for remodeling can be divided roughly into three stages:

1. Preparation and Rough Construction.
2. Closing in the New Work.
3. Finishing the Work.

The following pages outline the basic steps in each stage of construction and *The Construction Process* diagram summarizes them. The steps will overlap, but the amount of overlap will vary among projects. Building inspections are listed at the approximate intervals when they might occur; actual times will be determined by your local building department. (Your contractor's outline and schedule may contain much more detail.) If you want to know more about construction, there are many books available on the subject. Some are listed in the *Resources* section. In addition, your contractor can answer questions about the construction process.

During construction, the contractor will request payments as per the contract. Before you (or the lender) pay the contractor, the designer and you must decide if the contractor's payment request matches the amount of work completed. Keep copies of all payment requests, invoices and cancelled checks for your records and balance them against the total contract while work proceeds. You can use the *Payments to the Contractor* form to keep track. Remember to withhold 10 percent of each payment if your contract specifies "retention." Always get a proper receipt if you pay cash. NEVER PAY FOR WORK WHICH HAS NOT BEEN DONE! If you purchase materials yourself, use the *Materials Expenses* worksheet to record your purchases.

As stated earlier, keeping track of progress and changes during this phase is especially important. There are several *Construction Meeting Memo* forms at the end of this chapter for you to use. You also may want to take photographs.

Construction usually begins with a flurry of activity!

☞ The construction process starts with site preparation and/or demolition. The area where construction will take place (whether it is inside or outside) must be cleared and made ready. It may require removal of shrubs and concrete patios or exterior and interior walls. Demolition is quick, dirty and noisy. (Sometimes existing exterior walls are not removed until a new room is enclosed.) Make certain that the contractor knows where to stop.

Demolition may reveal that some assumptions were incorrect about structural supports, plumbing and other conditions hidden in walls. If so, changes may have to be made. As noted before, it is difficult to avoid this type of change.

☞ Materials will be delivered to the site. Examples are framing lumber, reinforcing steel and plywood.

☞ If a new room is being added, trenches must be dug for foundations and the entire area under the new construction will be excavated as required (from a few inches for a concrete slab to several feet for a basement). Forms will be built and reinforcing steel will be placed for the new foundations.

☛ Building Inspection - of foundation forms and reinforcing steel.

☞ Then the foundation will be built, usually of concrete or concrete block.

☞ You may begin to receive "preliminary lien notices" in the mail. Remember, these mean ONLY that a subcontractor or material supplier is working on your project.

☞ After construction of foundations, framing for the floors will be built.

☞ Work that will be concealed under the floor will be completed (plumbing, electrical, heating and ventilation.)

☛ Building Inspection - of underfloor work.

☞ The subfloor or rough floor will be laid.

☞ Then the walls, second floor (if there is one), roof and ceilings will be framed. This is called rough framing. It can be erected very quickly but it must be straight and solid to be a good base for the finishes that will be applied. When rough framing has been completed, you will see the shape of your rooms.

☛ Building Inspection - of framing.

At this stage, the building process seems to slow down because the changes are less dramatic. More individual subcontractors or trades will participate for short periods of time. Scheduling will become like a juggling act for the general contractor. He or she will be coordinating the schedules of several small businesses - the electrician, the plumber, the heating contractor and others. If the overall schedule is a day or two behind, a crucial subcontractor may not be able to work when necessary.

☞ Exterior wall and roof sheathing will be installed everywhere except at windows and doors. Sheathing usually is made in 4 foot by 8 foot sheets and the type varies (insulation board, plywood, exterior gypsum board and others).

☛ Building inspections may be required at several points during this period depending on the local building department.

☞ Then carpenters will install window frames and exterior doors. Sometimes glass is installed later.

☞ While the sheathing, doors and windows are being installed, the electrician, plumber and heating contractor will return to do work within the walls and ceilings. (It may appear that they are destroying the framing because they often cut holes in supporting members to install wires and pipes.) Most building codes define what may and may not be cut. Building inspectors will review the work, but if the work looks wrong to you, ask the contractor if it is correct.

☞ The exterior wall finish (siding or plaster) will be installed.

☞ Metal flashing for water protection will be installed.

☞ Then the roofing contractor will install new roofing.

☛ Building Inspection - for all work to be concealed within the walls.

☞ Insulation will be installed in the exterior walls and roof or ceilings, if insulation board sheathing was not used or is insufficient to meet code requirements.

☞ Gypsum wallboard (or another material) will be installed to close in all interior walls. Usually 4 foot by 8 or 10 foot sheets are used.

☛ Building Inspection - for nailing of gypsum wallboard.

☞ The joints of the gypsum wallboard will be taped, sanded and textured to obtain an even surface. This is a MESSY and time consuming task. Surfaces must dry before they can be sanded. If the weather is cold or damp, drying takes longer. Sanding creates large quantities of fine dust which migrates everywhere. (Inspect your belongings to make certain that they are protected. The general contractor should cover openings between the remodeled area and rooms which are unchanged.) The process is repeated until surfaces are even enough to receive final finishes.

Like many projects, the last 10 percent of a remodeling seems to take 50 percent of the time. Once again, several of the subcontractors must return to complete their work (install light fixtures, plumbing fixtures, wood trim, etc.) Sometimes one subcontractor can not finish until another is done. And sometimes fixtures and finish items will arrive late.

There may be decisions yet to make during this stage, too. Detail items such as cabinet pulls, color of switch plates and paint colors are often selected during construction. Make your decisions expeditiously so the work can be completed. Small items can always be changed later if you really do not like them. You can even repaint a room at another time. On the other hand, if you feel that all the decisions require thinking time, take the time and be comfortable. But realize that your project may not be completed as quickly.

☞ Carpenters will install all door and window trim, moldings, etc.

☞ Cabinets will be installed.

☞ Paint and wallpaper will be applied. Usually interior paint is applied first (walls, trim and cabinets.) Then exterior work is completed.

Note: It is VERY difficult to select paint colors from tiny chips. The final paint application is affected by sunlight and shadow, color of adjacent surfaces, type of paint (flat, semi-gloss or glossy finish) and texture of the surface to be painted. Make certain that you approve sample paint colors applied by the painter in the correct locations before final painting begins. Paint samples should be large enough to show the colors accurately. Place other materials (carpet, drapery and upholstery fabric) next to the sample to see the total effect.

☞ The electrician, plumber and heating contractor will install fixtures, switch plates, ventilation grilles and other finish work.

☞ Flooring (hardwood, sheet vinyl, ceramic tile) will be installed.

Note: It is a good idea for someone (the architect, the contractor or you) to supervise the installation of finishes which have patterns or which must be aligned in a specific way. There is a Murphy's Law about finishes: the installer will always apply finishes differently from the way you visualized them.

☞ Countertops will be installed.

☞ Appliances will be installed.

☞ Finish hardware (cabinet pulls, door knobs), mirrors and shower doors will be installed.

☞ Carpeting will be laid.

☞ FINAL BUILDING INSPECTION - the building inspector verifies that all community requirements have been met.

Making Changes During Construction

Follow a standard procedure for making changes during construction. It will prevent misunderstandings between the contractor and you. Remember that any time you ask your contractor to do something different from the original contract, IT MAY COST MORE MONEY AND IT MAY TAKE MORE TIME. (Although it may be obvious that some small changes will not affect price or time, it is never wrong to ask.) Your designer can help make changes and document them. A basic procedure is the following:

Ask for a price quote.

Whenever you want to make a change, ask the contractor to quote a price for the work and to estimate if the project will take more time to complete. Also ask if the change will affect any other elements of the project. Occasionally you will need to ask the designer to prepare additional drawings to illustrate the change.

Put the change in writing.

When you have agreed upon the change, put it in writing. It will become part of the contract and may affect the total contract price (increase OR decrease) and/or the time schedule. Your change order document should state:

- Name of the owner and project.
- Name of the contractor.
- Reference to inclusion in original contract dated _____.
- Description of change.
- Change in contract price and new total price.
- Change in contract time.

You, the contractor and the designer (if appropriate) should sign and date this statement of change. Your designer may have "Change Order" forms to use or you can purchase them from the American Institute of Architects. Keep your copies of all Change Orders with your original contract.

Helping to Prevent Problems During Construction

By this time you have already done two of the most important things that help prevent problems from occurring. They are:

- Stay organized throughout the project.

• Hire a reliable and responsible contractor.

Other measures to take are:

• Observe the construction area every day, but do not get in the way of construction. If something does not look right, don't be afraid to ask questions of the contractor (or the designer if appropriate.) Remember to direct your questions to the contractor's representative.

• If you make a change, be certain to put it in writing before the contractor starts to implement the change. See the above section on making changes for more detail.

• Check the contractor's schedule regularly and ask questions if you see that construction progress is different from the schedule. Be firm about staying on schedule, but be understanding if there are good reasons for delay (strikes, rain, unavailable materials). Often a lagging schedule can be brought back on target, but sometimes unavoidable problems extend the schedule.

• If you have decisions to make during construction, make them as quickly as possible so as not to delay the work.

What If There are Problems with the Contractor?

Sometimes there will be problems with the contractor despite careful planning.

• If problems arise, your designer or you should talk to the contractor immediately. Many problems can be resolved and most contractors are very willing to make corrections.

• If the contractor refuses to make corrections, you can file a written complaint with your local Contractors' State License Board. The Board will investigate valid complaints against contractors and discipline the contractor if necessary. This process may take time.

• If corrections still are not made, consult your legal counsel. Determine what might be appropriate legal action considering the magnitude of the problem.

• Another alternative is to arrange arbitration proceedings, as per your contract.

• If you have a performance bond and your contractor abandons the job, your bond will insure that the job will be completed as per contract.

Closing Out the Project

It is important to hold inspections and complete paperwork at the end of the project, too. These final steps help assure that there will be no problems after the contractor finishes construction. They are described below. There is also a checklist in this chapter for *Completing the Project*. Remember that you should not make your final payment to the contractor until EVERYTHING is complete.

Inspecting the Project

When your remodeling project is nearly finished, you should meet with the designer and the contractor for a thorough inspection of the work. The contractor will prepare a list of all items yet to be completed (a "punch list" or inspection list). Typically punch list items will be small things like installing hardware, touching up paint or replacing trim. You or the designer may add to the list while you review the project.

If everyone agrees that the work is "substantially complete" (the project is sufficiently complete according to contract that you can move in and occupy it for its intended use), the architect will prepare a "Certificate of Substantial Completion". The punch list will be attached and dates will be set when you can move in and when all items on the punch list must be finished. The date of substantial completion sets the beginning of warranty periods for all construction work except those items on the punch list. Punch list item warranties begin on the date of final payment. The owner, the contractor and the designer should sign the Certificate of Substantial Completion and it should be filed with your city or county.

Occupancy Permit

Some communities require the owner to obtain a "Certificate of Occupancy" or "Occupancy Permit" before using new rooms. Usually the owner will apply, but often the contractor must show compliance with all community requirements (pass the final building inspection) before the permit will be issued. Check with your community to see if one is required.

Obtain Owner Information from the Contractor

Ask the contractor for the following:

- Owners' manuals (operating instructions) for equipment and appliances.
- Keys for all locking doors.
- All guarantees required by the contract.
- Maintenance instructions for finishes (walls, floors, countertops).

Moving In

At this point you can finally .... MOVE IN!!! Start to enjoy your remodeled home and the results of your careful planning efforts.

Final Inspection

When ALL the work has been completed, the contractor, the designer and you will hold a final inspection. If everything is done according to contract, you should send a letter to the contractor stating that everything is complete and acceptable.

Lien Releases.

The contractor must satisfy the requirements for "release of liens" as per your contract BEFORE you make final payment for construction. As stated earlier (see Chapter 7), lien releases verify that subcontractors and materials suppliers have been paid by the general contractor and the subcontractors and suppliers relinquish the right of filing liens against your property. (The contractor probably will request final payment before he or she provides lien release documentation.)

Final Payment

After you and your designer are satisfied that the contractor has completed ALL contractual obligations including release of liens, you should make final payment to the contractor. Final payment covers all retention withheld throughout the job and all work including that added by change order. Final payment may be made after the 30 to 60 day lien period has elapsed. ∎

The Construction Process

Before Construction Begins

Completing the paperwork and preparing for construction.

- △ Completing the paperwork.
  - • Financing.
  - • Insurance coverage.
  - • Construction contract.
  - • Building permit and subpermits.
- △ Have a preconstruction meeting with the contractor.
- △ Make final plans for the household.
- • Prepare your home, your family, yourself and plan diversions.

Preparation and Rough Construction

Getting rid of existing walls, roof, etc. that will be replaced and starting the new construction - foundations, floor framing, wiring, etc.

- △ Site preparation and demolition.
- △ Dig and prepare for foundation.
- * BUILDING INSPECTION.
- △ Build foundation.
- △ Frame the floors.
- • Install underfloor plumbing and electrical.
- * BUILDING INSPECTION.
- △ Lay subfloor.
- △ Frame walls, roof and ceilings.
- * BUILDING INSPECTION.

Closing In the New Work

Applying wall and roof finishes; installing doors and windows; and installing all the wiring, plumbing, etc. that will be hidden in the walls and ceilings.

- △ Apply exterior wall and roof sheathing.
- △ Install window frames and exterior doors.
- • More electrical and plumbing work.
- △ Apply exterior wall finish.
- △ Apply flashing and roofing.
- * BUILDING INSPECTION.
- △ Install insulation.
- △ Apply wallboard.
- * BUILDING INSPECTION.
- △ Tape wallboard.

Finishing the Work

Completing installation of all floor, wall and ceiling finishes; installing cabinets, countertops and appliances; adding trim, light fixtures, switches and hardware.

- △ Install door and window trim.
- △ Install cabinets.
- △ Apply paint and wallpaper.
- △ Finish plumbing, electrical.
- △ Install flooring.
- △ Install countertops.
- △ Install appliances.
- △ Install hardware.
- △ Install carpeting.
- * FINAL INSPECTION.

Closing Out the Project

Inspecting the project and completing the the paperwork that finishes the contract.

- △ Inspect the project.
- △ Occupancy permit?
- △ Obtain owner info.
- * MOVE IN.
- △ Final inspection.
- △ Lien releases.
- △ Final payment to contractor.

Month 5 | Month 6 | Month 7 | Month 8 | Month 9

Preconstruction Checklist

Review these items before the contractor begins work.

- **Finish the paperwork.**
    - Complete financing arrangements.
    - Arrange for additional property insurance coverage.
    - Sign construction contract.
    - Obtain building permit and subpermits (usually done by contractor.)

- **Have a preconstruction meeting among owner, architect and contractor.**
  (Discuss the following.)
    - Who is contractor's representative?
    - How can you reach the contractor in case of emergency after hours?
    - Schedule a regular job meeting to review progress and questions.
    - When must you make any remaining decisions?
    - Review:
        Work schedule.

        Contractor's work hours.

        Where to bring materials and equipment onto the property.

        Where to store materials and equipment on the property.

        Limits of construction area.

        Daily clean-up requirements.

        Security requirements for construction area and house.

        Procedures for making changes.

        Contractor's submittal of invoices.

- **Make final plans for the family.**
    - Prepare your home.
    - Prepare your family.
    - Prepare yourself.
    - Plan diversions.

Payments to the Contractor

Keep track of payments to the contractor on this worksheet.

BASIC CONTRACT AMOUNT $_____

ADDITIONS TO THE CONTRACT

Addition Number	Date	Amount		Subtotal
_____	_/_/_	$_____		Subtotal $_____
_____	_/_/_	$_____		$_____
_____	_/_/_	$_____		$_____
_____	_/_/_	$_____		$_____

Payment Number	Date	Payment Amount	Retention	Paid to Date	Amount Remaining
_____	_/_/_	$_____	$_____	$_____	$_____
_____	_/_/_	$_____	$_____	$_____	$_____
_____	_/_/_	$_____	$_____	$_____	$_____
_____	_/_/_	$_____	$_____	$_____	$_____
_____	_/_/_	$_____	$_____	$_____	$_____
_____	_/_/_	$_____	$_____	$_____	$_____
_____	_/_/_	$_____	$_____	$_____	$_____
_____	_/_/_	$_____	$_____	$_____	$_____
_____	_/_/_	$_____	$_____	$_____	$_____
_____	_/_/_	$_____	$_____	$_____	$_____

Total Retention $_____

FINAL PAYMENT   _/_/_ $_____ $_____

TOTAL CONSTRUCTION CONTRACT PAYMENT AMOUNT $_____

Direct Materials Expenses

Keep track of materials that you purchase directly from suppliers on this Worksheet.

Date	Item and Supplier	Amount Paid	Amount Remaining	Total Cost
/ /	_____	$ _____	$ _____	
	_____	$ _____	$ _____	
	_____	$ _____	$ _____	$ _____
/ /	_____	$ _____	$ _____	
	_____	$ _____	$ _____	
	_____	$ _____	$ _____	$ _____
/ /	_____	$ _____	$ _____	
	_____	$ _____	$ _____	
	_____	$ _____	$ _____	$ _____
/ /	_____	$ _____	$ _____	
	_____	$ _____	$ _____	
	_____	$ _____	$ _____	$ _____
/ /	_____	$ _____	$ _____	
	_____	$ _____	$ _____	
	_____	$ _____	$ _____	$ _____
/ /	_____	$ _____	$ _____	
	_____	$ _____	$ _____	
	_____	$ _____	$ _____	$ _____
/ /	_____	$ _____	$ _____	
	_____	$ _____	$ _____	
	_____	$ _____	$ _____	$ _____
/ /	_____	$ _____	$ _____	
	_____	$ _____	$ _____	
	_____	$ _____	$ _____	$ _____
/ /	_____	$ _____	$ _____	
	_____	$ _____	$ _____	
	_____	$ _____	$ _____	$ _____

GRAND TOTAL $ _____

Completing the Project

Some of the items to complete at the end of construction include:

- **Inspect all new work before moving into the remodeled spaces.**
    - Prepare Certificate of Substantial Completion.
    - With contractor, compile Punch List (or inspection list) of work yet to be completed.

- **Obtain Occupancy Permit, if required by your community.**

- **Obtain owner information from contractor.**
    - Owners' manuals for equipment and appliances.
    - Keys for all doors.
    - Guarantees.
    - Maintenance instructions for materials and surfaces.

- **MOVE IN!**

- **Complete FINAL Inspection.**
    - All Punch List items should be complete.
    - Send Letter of Completion to contractor.

- **Contractor provides lien release documentation as per contract and state requirements.**

- **Make final payment to contractor.**
    - Make final payment to the contractor AFTER you are satisfied that absolutely everything is complete and acceptable.

Construction Job Meeting Memo

Date _____

Attending:

    Name   **Representing**

_____   _____

_____   _____

_____   _____

_____   _____

Items Covered:

1. _____

    _____

2. _____

    _____

3. _____

    _____

4. _____

    _____

	Person Responsible:	**Date for Answer**
Action for Next Meeting:		
1.	_____	_____
2.	_____	_____
3.	_____	_____
4.	_____	_____
5.	_____	_____
6.	_____	_____

Changes:	**Cost**	**Time**
1.	_____	_____
2.	_____	_____
3.	_____	_____
4.	_____	_____

Construction Job Meeting Memo

Date _____

Attending:

Name	Representing
_____	_____
_____	_____
_____	_____

Items Covered:

1. _____
_____
2. _____
_____
3. _____
_____
4. _____
_____

Action for Next Meeting:	**Person Responsible:**	**Date for Answer**
1. _____	_____	_____
_____		
2. _____	_____	_____
_____		
3. _____	_____	_____
_____		
4. _____	_____	_____
_____		
5. _____	_____	_____
_____		
6. _____	_____	_____
_____		

Changes:	**Cost**	**Time**
1. _____	_____	_____
2. _____	_____	_____
3. _____	_____	_____
4. _____	_____	_____

Construction Job Meeting Memo

Date _____

Attending:

Name	Representing
_____	_____
_____	_____
_____	_____
_____	_____

Items Covered:

1. _____
_____
2. _____
_____
3. _____
_____
4. _____
_____

Action for Next Meeting:

		Person Responsible:	Date for Answer
1. _____		_____	_____
_____			
2. _____		_____	_____
_____			
3. _____		_____	_____
_____			
4. _____		_____	_____
_____			
5. _____		_____	_____
_____			
6. _____		_____	_____
_____			

Changes:

	Cost	Time
1. _____	_____	_____
2. _____	_____	_____
3. _____	_____	_____
4. _____	_____	_____

9

ACTION.

POTENTIAL PROBLEMS AND PITFALLS.

☛Investigate furnishings thoroughly before you purchase or order. You will be more likely to get what you want.

☛If you order furnishings, delivery may take a long time.

☛Order from reliable sources.

☛If furnishings are damaged when they are delivered, report it immediately to the seller.

Furnishings

Although furnishings are the last element of this book, it was recommended in earlier chapters that you consider the furnishings to be an integral part of your project from the early design stages. They affect both your budget and the overall floor plans of your remodeling. Furnishings also satisfy the final functional requirements and complete the character of your project. An illustration is that a durable, comfortable sofa and lounge chairs, a spacious coffee table and good reading lamps can make a family room usable and comfortable. Contemporary furniture and light colors can give it a spacious active feeling, while traditional furniture and dark colors can make it feel quiet, cozy and calm.

Selecting Furnishings

Selection of furnishings (style, size, material, color and texture) depends YOUR taste, YOUR needs and YOUR budget. Your rooms should express your own personality and lifestyle, not that of someone else. Although you may find good ideas in home design magazines and friends may give you advice, be sure to use only those ideas that truly fit your own style and needs. You and your family must be satisfied living with the style and the furnishings that you select.

Many homeowners select furnishings themselves, but some hire design consultants (see Chapter 5) to interpret their needs and assist with interior design and furniture selection. If you hire a designer, some choices are:

- Interior designers.
- Architects.
- Furniture or department stores.
  (Many stores provide design assistance as part of the cost of the furnishings if you purchase from them. Select a store that you trust and that has a reputation for providing good service.)

If you would like additional information before you decide about design help, there are numerous books available about interior design and furnishings. Some are listed in the *Resources* section. These books can also help you define your own style.

Alternative Approaches

Since most furniture must be ordered at least a few weeks in advance, there are two basic ways to approach selection of furnishings. (This is true whether you select them yourself or you hire a designer.)

Select and order furnishings during the design process.
- Consider your furniture needs during plan design. Shop for furnishings to learn what is available. (See the next section.)
- Plan the furniture and rooms to work together as a complete design. Select the major pieces of furniture and draw them on a floor plan. If you are working with an interior designer or architect, he or she will draw the plan and list the specifications.
- Order the furnishings during the design or construction phase. The furnishings should be delivered by the time you are ready to move into your new rooms, although sometimes there are delays. If furniture arrives early, most stores and designers will arrange for storage. You can select accessories (lamps, art objects, bookcases) during design or after you move in.

Select and order furnishings after construction is complete.
- You can wait until construction is finished to make final selection of furnishings, but you should make initial plans during the design process. Give the same planning consideration as above.
- Prepare a floor plan showing representative furnishings.
- However, do not order the furnishings. After you have moved in, live in the rooms briefly and then order furnishings. You can experiment with existing furniture to help clarify your ideas and make final decisions. Be prepared to wait (sometimes as long as six months after you order) until everything arrives.

Purchasing Furnishings

Background

Most consumer products are produced under brand names and are distributed by multiple local retailers. An abundance of information about the products is available for consumers to review and compare. Consumers can visit any shopping center, walk through upbeat stores with eye-catching displays and take new purchases home immediately. Many products can be returned if they are unsatisfactory.

The furnishings industry is almost the opposite:

- There are few brands of American furniture that consumers would recognize. It has been accepted practice for furniture retailers to cover manufacturers' labels with their own.

- One third of American furniture retailers ceased operating between 1979 and 1983 due primarily to recession and high interest rates. "Design centers" and design showrooms which are open "only to the trade" (interior designers and architects) house many of the best furniture designs. Part of the design profession has encouraged "only to the trade" showrooms for two reasons: they claim that the public needs designers to educate them about furnishings, and many designers earn their fees from markups on net furniture prices.

- Although a wide variety of furniture is sold in the United States, little consumer information is available about quality and construction.

- Because furnishings do not turn over as rapidly as many consumer goods, displays of furnishings are changed infrequently, are often uninspiring compared to other retail displays and do not incorporate our contemporary lifestyles (low maintenance materials, use of home electronics and home offices).

- It is rare that you can walk into a furniture store, purchase a piece of furniture and take it home with you or have it delivered quickly. Ordering furniture may take up to six months, even from large department stores. Furniture often is built to fill specific orders and there may be many orders ahead of yours. Typically, you can not return furniture if it is unsatisfactory.

However, things are beginning to change. Brand name images are appearing. Some brand name manufacturers are hiring noted designers to promote and update their lines of furniture. (Ralph Lauren recently introduced his first furniture collection.) Others are strengthening their images with nationwide distribution in their own stores (Ethan Allen and Thomasville) and offering more furnishings and better services to the public. Newer chains are offering well-designed and well-priced contemporary furnishings throughout the country. A few new specialty stores offer unique international designs to everyone. Although for the most part design centers are still only open to the trade, interior designers and architects can purchase for the general public at design centers. The public also can purchase furnishings from discounters in North Carolina where much American furniture is manufactured. However, it still tends to take several weeks for delivery when you special order furniture.

Shopping for Furnishings

You will probably live with your furnishings a long time, perhaps longer than you live with your home. Take your floor plan and list of furnishings that you are considering and visit showrooms and stores to learn what is available. If you are working with a designer, he or she will guide you through the showrooms or recommend stores to visit. Even if you order from a catalog, it is wise to see similar furnishings in-person before you make decisions about purchasing. You are less likely to be unpleasantly surprised if you have examined a similar item.

Sources for purchasing furnishings.

You can purchase furnishings from a variety of sources. Large cities, of course, offer a greater selection. You will find a wide range of prices for similar items and delivery prices also may vary significantly. Some manufacturers and retailers offer written warranties, but many do not. Basic sources are listed below.

- Department Stores.
  Many large department stores sell a complete range of furnishings and some offer design assistance.

- Furniture Stores.
  These stores typically have been local or regional retailers but now include a growing number of chains which market attractive and competitively priced furnishings. Some furniture manufacturers also have stores throughout the country. Many furniture stores also will help you with design.

  Local antique dealers who offer a range of American and European antiques are another source of furnishings.

- Design Centers and Design Showrooms.
  Design Centers are groups of design showrooms that usually display lines of high quality furnishings. Typically they are located in metropolitan areas. The showrooms represent one or more lines of furnishings and are open only to interior designers

and architects; the public has limited access when accompanied by designers or during special events.

In most cases, the public can not purchase directly from showrooms. Showrooms sell to designers at "net" price, and designers resell to the public at a marked-up price, usually retail or "list" price which is 80% to 100% more. (Prices displayed at showrooms are "list" prices.) The markup has been a standard way for designers to bill their fees. Today designers charge a range of markup percentages (from 10% to 100%) depending on the amount of work they do, or they may bill you net price plus handling costs and charge additional hourly rates for their design work.

- Designers.
Designers can purchase furnishings as described above. If you do not live near a design center, your local designers can order directly from showrooms in other communities.

- Furniture Catalogs.
Spiegel and other catologs offer shoppers the convenience of purchasing by mail or telephone 24 hours a day.

- Mail Order Discounters.
Mail order discounters, particularily in North Carolina, offer reduced prices to buyers because they typically order directly from the manufacturer. However, sometimes the prices are not much better than the best local prices. Drawbacks are that time delays may be greater, defective furniture and shipping damage problems are difficult to solve and it may be impossible to get a deposit back if you want to cancel an order. Mail order firms often advertise in home design magazines.

Finding local sources.
Since many advertise liberally, finding local sources for furnishings is more direct than finding designers and contractors. It is important to get good recommendations about furniture sources, too. A store is not necessarily good just because it is large. In addition to quality merchandise, you should look for prompt delivery, customer service and a good record of correcting problems. Ask friends for recommendations and check with local consumer groups. Sometimes consumer groups evaluate regional stores. (Check the telephone directory or the library for consumer group listings.)

You can find names of sources from the following:

- Friends and business acquaintances.
- Advertisements in local newspapers and magazines. (Look for descriptions of what is sold at each store so you can eliminate stores inappropriate for your needs and taste.)
- The Yellow Pages of your telephone directory.

Examining furnishings.
Use the *Furnishings Checklist* to examine the items that you like. Look at construction and ask about durability and maintenance. Sit on chairs and sofas; lie down on beds; sit at tables; and open all operable parts of cabinets. Ask to see catalog descriptions and specifications and obtain copies if you can. When you examine upholstered goods, look at:
- Frames.
- Springs and padding.
- Cushions.
- Fabric.
- Trim.

When you examine case goods (tables, bookcases, desks, cabinets), look at:
- Drawers.
- Doors and lids.
- Legs.
- Finishes.
- Hardware.

Other information you should learn is:
- Size of furnishings. Measure the furnishings yourself or ask for dimensions. (They must fit your rooms.)
- Ask the price of each item and the terms of payment. Is a deposit required? Is delivery cost extra? Compare prices among stores if possible.
- Find out the typical delivery time.
- Ask if there is a warranty. Typically furniture manufacturers do not provide written warranties like those you receive with appliances or electronic equipment. Retailers normally do not provide them either, but often retailers will correct problems.

Making Purchases

When you are ready to order, review your list of purchases, prices, terms of payment and all important information with the seller. Obtain a copy of the order form for your records. Often you will be required to make a 50% deposit when you place your order, but you may be able to negotiate a smaller deposit.

If you purchase stock items from a retailer, your furnishings may be delivered in a few weeks. If you special order, delivery often takes three to six months. Ask for an estimated delivery date and request the salesperson to contact you when he or she receives confirmation from the manufacturer. (Most manufacturers send written confirmations to retailers within three or four weeks of the order stating factory estimated delivery dates.) If the seller will agree, it is a good idea to have the right to cancel your order should the seller learn that the factory estimated delivery date is significantly later than the original estimate. Halfway through the order period, call the seller to verify that the delivery date is still the same. Check again when the date draws near. At this point if the date continues to move back, you probably can not do anything about it. But if you are persistent, you <u>may</u> be able to get a response.

Use the *Purchasing Furnishings* form to keep track of your purchases from ordering through delivery. There is also a *Payments for Furnishings* form where you may want to record your expenditures for furnishings.

Inspect Furnishings When they are Delivered

Typically furnishings will be delivered to your home when they arrive. You should do the following:

- Check immediately for flaws and damage. It is best to inspect your purchases while the delivery person waits. If there is a defect, note it on the delivery slip and contact the seller to remedy the problem. If the defect is major, you may want to reject the furniture.
- If you notice a defect later, contact the seller immediately.
- Promptly send a written statement explaining any defects to the seller.

Furnishings Checklist

Consider these factors when selecting furnishings.

- **Quality and Durability.**
    - Is it made well?
        (Look at seams, joints, material, fabric, operation of drawers, etc.)
    - Is it durable enough for your planned use?
        (Frequent use by children, use by adults, infrequent use.)
    - How long do you want it to last?
    - Is there a warranty?

- **Style and purpose.**
    - Does the style fit your design goals?
    - Does the furniture suit your purpose?
        (Is the table big enough? Does the dresser have enough drawers?)
    - Is it comfortable for the user?

- **Size.**
    - Will this piece of furniture fit where you want to put it? (Measure it.)
    - Can you move it to that location? (Through doorways, up stairs, etc.)

- **Maintenance.**
    - Are the finish and fabric easy to maintain?
    - Does the required maintenance fit into the time you have available for this chore?

- **Price.**
    - Does the price fit into your overall budget for furnishings?
    - Is a deposit required?
    - Is the cost of delivery extra?

- **Delivery.**
    - After you order, how long will it take until delivery?

Purchasing Furnishings

Use this form to keep track of furnishings that you purchase.

Furniture Store _____ Sales Person _____

Address _____ Phone No. _____

_____

Description of Item:

_____

_____

Materials _____

Quantity	Manufacturer	Catalog No.	Size	Color
_____	_____	_____	_____	_____

Base Cost	Tax	Delivery Cost	Other	Total Cost
$_____	$_____	$_____	$_____	$_____

Warranty Yes No	Order Date	Estimated Delivery	Reconfirm On	Reconfirm Again
____ ____	___/___/___	___/___/___	___/___/___	___/___/___

Description of Item:

_____

_____

Materials _____

Quantity	Manufacturer	Catalog No.	Size	Color
_____	_____	_____	_____	_____

Base Cost	Tax	Delivery Cost	Other	Total Cost
$_____	$_____	$_____	$_____	$_____

Warranty Yes No	Order Date	Estimated Delivery	Reconfirm On	Reconfirm Again
____ ____	___/___/___	___/___/___	___/___/___	___/___/___

Purchasing Furnishings

Use this form to keep track of furnishings that you purchase.

Furniture Store _____   Sales Person _____

Address   _____   Phone No.   _____

                _____

Description of Item:

_____

_____

Materials   _____

Quantity	Manufacturer	Catalog No.	Size	Color
_____	_____	_____	_____	_____

Base Cost	Tax	Delivery Cost	Other	Total Cost
$_____	$_____	$_____	$_____	$_____

Warranty Yes No	Order Date	Estimated Delivery	Reconfirm On	Reconfirm Again
____ ____	___/___/___	___/___/___	___/___/___	___/___/___

Description of Item:

_____

_____

Materials   _____

Quantity	Manufacturer	Catalog No.	Size	Color
_____	_____	_____	_____	_____

Base Cost	Tax	Delivery Cost	Other	Total Cost
$_____	$_____	$_____	$_____	$_____

Warranty Yes No	Order Date	Estimated Delivery	Reconfirm On	Reconfirm Again
____ ____	___/___/___	___/___/___	___/___/___	___/___/___

Payments for Furnishings

Keep track of furnishings purchases on this Worksheet.

Date	Item and Store	Amount Paid	Amount Remaining	Total Cost
/ /	_____	$ _____	$ _____	
	_____	$ _____	$ _____	
	_____	$ _____	$ _____	$ _____
/ /	_____	$ _____	$ _____	
	_____	$ _____	$ _____	
	_____	$ _____	$ _____	$ _____
/ /	_____	$ _____	$ _____	
	_____	$ _____	$ _____	
	_____	$ _____	$ _____	$ _____
/ /	_____	$ _____	$ _____	
	_____	$ _____	$ _____	
	_____	$ _____	$ _____	$ _____
/ /	_____	$ _____	$ _____	
	_____	$ _____	$ _____	
	_____	$ _____	$ _____	$ _____
/ /	_____	$ _____	$ _____	
	_____	$ _____	$ _____	
	_____	$ _____	$ _____	$ _____
/ /	_____	$ _____	$ _____	
	_____	$ _____	$ _____	
	_____	$ _____	$ _____	$ _____
/ /	_____	$ _____	$ _____	
	_____	$ _____	$ _____	
	_____	$ _____	$ _____	$ _____
/ /	_____	$ _____	$ _____	
	_____	$ _____	$ _____	
	_____	$ _____	$ _____	$ _____

GRAND TOTAL $ _____

Notes

Glossary

This glossary is a guide to architectural terms and other words that you may want to know during your home remodeling project. They will help you communicate with the Building Department, your designer and your contractor. Additional terms and more extensive definitions can be found in books listed in the *Resources* section.

ARBITRATION CLAUSE A statement in a contract which provides that claims or disputes may be settled by an arbitrator or panel of arbitrators rather than by litigation.

BASEBOARD A molding which covers the joint between a wall and the floor.

BEAM A principal horizontal load bearing member of a structure. Beams usually support other smaller structural members.

BUILDING DEPARTMENT The local government regulatory agency which provides information about local requirements for construction, issues building permits and monitors construction.

BUILDING PERMIT Permission for construction granted by the local government regulatory agency. The usual procedure is to file a written application and to pay a fee (often based on estimated construction cost). A building permit is usually required for demolition, new construction, remodeling, expansion, addition or repair to any structure, but not for maintenance projects such as painting.

BUILT-UP ROOF A flat roof made of layers of waterproof papers and tars and covered with gravel.

CALCULATIONS Mathematical analysis of a building. The two types of calculations usually associated with house construction are:

> ENERGY CALCULATIONS Analysis of the energy loss and gain of a building to show that it is designed to meet state or local requirments for energy conservation.

> STRUCTURAL CALCULATIONS Analysis of the structural systems of a building to show that it is designed to meet local building code requirements.

CHANGE ORDER A legal change to a contract which changes the contract sum and/or the contract time.

CONSTRUCTION DOCUMENTS The drawings and specifications from which a contractor makes a bid and builds.

DESIGN/BUILD A term indicating that a single party or company can both design and build a construction project.

DOOR TYPES Doors can be described by the way they operate, the way they are built or their appearance. Often all three are combined to specify a door.

The way they operate:

BI-FOLD DOOR Hinged door panels that slide in an overhead track. Usually used for closets.

BY-PASS or SLIDING DOORS Doors which are hung from an overhead track and slide in front of each other along a floor guide to open. Usually used for closets.

POCKET SLIDING DOOR Door which is hung in an overhead track and slides into a "pocket" within the wall. Usually used where there is not enough space for a swinging door.

SWINGING or HINGED DOOR Door which is hinged on the side and swings into a room when it is open. Used for either exterior or interior locations.

The way they are built:

HOLLOW CORE DOOR Door which has an interior of honey-comb wood strips or corrugation and is covered with plywood and veneer. Used for interior locations.

PANEL or STILE AND RAIL DOOR Door with a wood frame composed of vertical (stile) and horizontal (rail) members and wood or glass panels set into the frame.

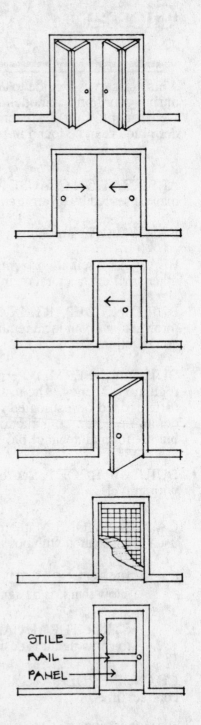

SOLID CORE DOOR Door which has an interior of wood blocking or particle board and is faced with veneer. Used for exterior locations or for sound or fire resistance.

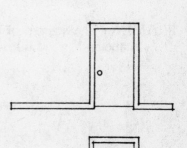

Their appearance:
FLUSH DOOR Door with a completely flat surface.

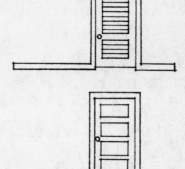

LOUVERED DOOR Panel door with louvers.

PANEL DOOR Door having one or more separate panels which are recessed into the door frame.

DOWNSPOUT A pipe which carries rainwater from the gutter of a roof to the ground.

DRAWINGS or PLANS The two-dimensional diagrams which show the location, design and dimensions of a project. They are drawn to scale and may include the following:

SITE PLAN or PLOT PLAN Shows the entire property, the building (including changes) and all property information (building setbacks, easements, driveways etc.) required by the local regulatory agency. An additional site plan may be used to show landscape work.

FLOOR PLANS Show all floors of the building where new construction will be done and all changes that will be made. Additional floor plans are often included to show the locations of structural elements, electrical outlets and light fixtures, heating and air conditioning equipment and furniture.

ELEVATIONS Show the exterior and/or interior walls of the building and rooms where new construction will be done and changes will be made.

EAVES The lower edge of a roof which overhangs a wall.

FASCIA or FASCIA BOARD A horizontal board covering the rafter ends at the edge of a roof or covering the joint between the top of a wall and the projecting eaves.

FENESTRATION The arrangement of windows in the walls of buildings.

FLASHING Sheet metal or similar material that is applied on a structure to prevent water seepage, typically at the joints where two materials or surfaces meet such as between the roof and the chimney or where vent pipes come through the roof.

FOOTING The enlargement at the base of a foundation wall or column to help spread the load.

FRAMING The system of structural members that gives shape and strength to a building.

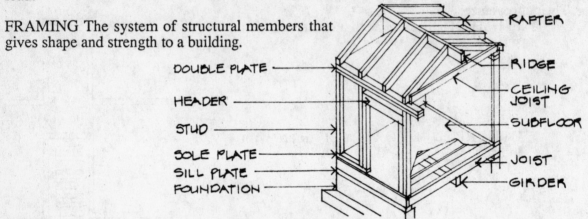

FURRING Narrow strips of wood or metal that are applied to a wall or another surface to make it level before applying the finish materials.

GIRDER A heavy beam which supports floor joists.

GUTTER A channel at the eaves of a roof that carries rainwater to downspouts.

HVAC An abbreviation for Heating, Ventilation and Air Conditioning.

HEADER A horizontal structural piece over a door opening, window opening or other opening in a wall. A header acts as a beam that supports loads from above and it must be supported by vertical members. Headers and their supports are usually concealed in walls.

JOIST Any of the parallel members that support a floor or ceiling. Joists are supported by walls or larger beams or girders. Joists are usually installed "on edge" - the narrow section of the joist bears on the wall or beam.

LIEN A legal claim placed by one person on the property of another to obtain payment for a debt or obligation.

LIQUIDATED DAMAGES An amount listed in the contract documents that is a "per day" assessment which the contractor must pay to the owner based on actual projected "per day" loss by the owner, if the project is not substantially complete on the date established in the contract. Actual loss must be proved. Usually applies to non-residential work.

MOLDING A decorative strip that is either carved into or applied to a surface. Often used around doors, windows or at the joint between walls and the ceiling.

MULLION A vertical member which separates and sometimes supports a series of windows, doors or panels.

OCCUPANCY The use of a building or its intended use.

PARAPET A low wall or railing which projects above the edge of a roof.

PERSPECTIVE DRAWING Shows a diagram of a building or room representing the relationship of objects as they might appear to the eye; shows a dimensional effect like a photograph. This type of drawing is often an extra service and is usually not included for construction bidding purposes.

PITCH The rate of incline or slope of a roof.

PUNCH LIST A list prepared near the end of the job (at Substantial Completion) which states items to be completed or corrected by the contractor to finish the project.

RAFTER Any one of the parallel load bearing members that support a roof.

RIDGE The peak of a roof where two sloping sides meet.

ROOF FORMS A roof may consist of a single form or a group of forms (either the same forms or a combination of different forms). The most common roof forms are the following:

FLAT ROOF A roof composed of a simple flat plane. It often has a slight slope for water drainage and may have a parapet wall along the edge for protection.

GABLE ROOF A roof composed of two sloping planes which begin at the top of walls on opposite sides of a building and slope up to meet at a peak or ridge.

GAMBREL ROOF A roof composed of four sloping planes, two on each side of the peak or ridge. The two planes slope at different angles with the lower plane having the steeper slope.

HIPPED ROOF A roof composed of four sloping planes which begin at the top of walls on four different sides of the building and slope up. The sloping diagonal joint where two planes meet is called a hip.

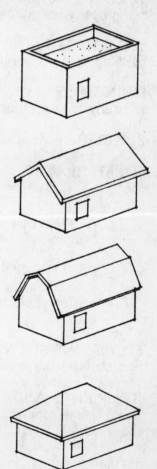

MANSARD ROOF A roof composed of eight sloping planes, two on each of the four different sides of a building. Like a gambrel roof, the two planes on each side slope at different angles with the lower plane having the steeper slope.

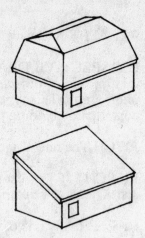

SHED ROOF A roof composed of a single sloping plane which slopes up from the top of a low wall to the top of a high wall.

SASH A window frame together with panes of glass.

SCALE The proportion between two different sets of dimensions. For architectural drawings, the relationship between the full scale of the original and the drawings.

SETBACK The required distance that a building must be built away from the front, side or rear property lines of a piece of property.

SHEATHING. The first layer of outside covering attached to wall studs or roof rafters of a building. It may be plywood, insulation board, etc.

SIDING A finish surface for exterior walls, usually wood or metal applied horizontally, vertically and sometimes diagonally.

SOFFIT The underside of an overhang on a building or in a room.

SOLAR HEATING and COOLING There are two ways that a building can use solar energy:

ACTIVE SOLAR Solar heating which uses a system of panels, hardware and other equipment to heat the building or to heat water for kitchen or bathroom use.

PASSIVE SOLAR Solar heating or cooling which uses the site, the building orientation, the building design, window orientation and thermal mass of floors and walls to help heat and cool the building. No system of panels and equipment is used.

SPECIFICATIONS A part of the construction documents consisting of written descriptions of materials, equipment, construction systems, standards and workmanship.

STAIR RISER AND TREAD The riser is the vertical board rising from the back of each step; the tread is the horizontal board spanning from riser to riser.

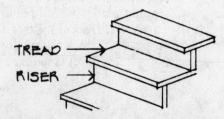

STUDS. The vertical framing members or supports in walls and partitions. In a home they are usually wood (often 2x4's), but they may also be metal.

SUBFLOOR The under layer of boards or plywood that is laid on joists. Finish flooring is installed over the subfloor.

SUBSTANTIAL COMPLETION The date established when the project is sufficiently complete according to the contract, that the owner may occupy the project for its intended use.

SURETY BONDS Bonds provide protection to the owner against loss resulting from the failure of contractors to perform according to the terms of the contract. Surety bonds allow the contractor to assure the owner that a project will be completed according to contract documents including payment for all labor and materials.
Types of surety bonds include:

> BID BOND A form of bid security; if the selected bidder cannot perform within a stipulated period of time, the difference between the selected bidder's proposal and the next acceptable bid (up to the amount of the bond) will be paid to the owner to assure that construction can be completed.

> LABOR AND MATERIALS BOND A surety bond which guarantees that the surety will pay all claimants for labor and materials used or reasonably required for use in performance of the contract. It helps provide protection against liens. Usually used with a Performance Bond.

> PERFORMANCE BOND A surety bond which quarantees that the project will be completed if the contractor defaults. Usually used with a Labor and Materials Bond.

THRESHOLD A wood or metal strip placed under an outside door.

VARIANCE Permission granted by a community allowing a person to build a structure that varies from community requirements. Usually granted in hardship cases only.

VENEER A thin sheet of material; often a layer of high quality wood applied over a layer of lower quality wood. Also a layer of brick or stone applied as a facing.

VENT A pipe or duct which directs undesirable air or gas out of a building.

WAINSCOT The lower three or four feet of an interior wall if finished differently from the rest of the wall.

WALL PLATES The horizontal framing members at the top and bottom of a wall. Studs are attached to and kept in place by the plates.

WINDOW TYPES Windows are typically classified by how they open. A window panel (frame together with panes of glass) is called a sash.

PARTS OF A WINDOW

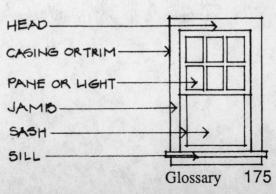

AWNING and HOPPER WINDOWS
Windows which are hinged at the top
(awning) or at the bottom (hopper). Awning
windows swing outward (and can provide
rain protection) and hopper windows swing
inward.

CASEMENT WINDOW A window which is
hinged at the side and swings outward.

CLERESTORY WINDOW A high window
located in a section of exterior wall which
rises above an adjacent roof. A clerestory
window may have fixed or movable sash.

DORMER WINDOW A window that rises
vertically above a sloping roof and is set
under a separate small roof.

DOUBLE-HUNG WINDOW A window
which has two sashes that slide vertically.

FIXED WINDOW A window which does
not open.

JALOUSIE WINDOW A window composed
of narrow horizontal slats which are held in
place at the sides and which operate like a
group of small awning windows. Jalousie
windows do not seal tightly.

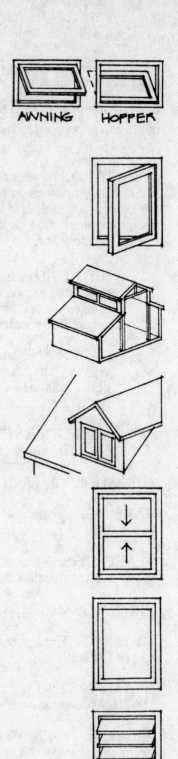

SINGLE-HUNG WINDOW Similar to a double-hung window, but one sash slides and one sash is fixed.

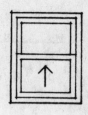

SLIDING WINDOW A window which has movable sash that slides horizontally and fixed sash. A sliding window may be composed of two, three or four panels.

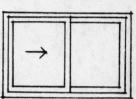

Notes

Resources

The following Resource pages list Information Sources and a Bibliography for home remodeling. Look for additional resources in the Yellow Pages of your telephone directory, at local home remodeling and design centers and at local bookstores.

Information Sources

These organizations and agencies usually will provide the informaton listed below their names and they may have other useful information, too. This listing typically indicates national offices, but there are local offices in many metropolitan areas.

AMERICAN INSTITUTE OF ARCHITECTS (AIA)
1735 New York Avenue N.W.
Washington, D.C. 20006

• Provides names of local member Architects who do residential work. (Local offices only.)
• Offers brochures, general information and sometimes books.
• Has contract forms available for purchase.

AMERICAN SOCIETY OF HOME INSPECTORS
655 15th Street NW., Suite 320
Washington D.C. 20005

• Information about membership and services.

AMERICAN SOCIETY OF INTERIOR DESIGNERS (ASID)
1430 Broadway
New York, New York 10018

• Provides names of local member Interior Designers who do design work for residences. (Local offices only.)

AMERICAN SOCIETY OF LANDSCAPE ARCHITECTS
1733 Connecticut Avenue N.W.
Washington, D.C. 20009

• Information about membership and services.

CONTRACTORS' STATE LICENSE BOARD
(May be listed under Consumer Complaint and Protection Coordinator or other consumer heading.) Usually located in the state capitol.

• Verifies if contractor is properly licensed and if license is in good standing.
• Answers inquiries regarding disciplinary action taken against a contractor by the Board.
• Accepts written complaints about contractors.
• Assists with and helps investigate all valid complaints against a contractor.
• Sometimes provides brochures.

NATIONAL ASSOCIATION OF HOME BUILDERS (NAHB)
Remodelers Council

15 and M Streets N.W.
Washington, D.C. 20005

• Brochure on working with contractors.
• Local office may provide names of local contractors.

NATIONAL TRUST FOR HISTORIC PRESERVATION

1100 Pennsylvania Avenue N.W., Suite 809
Washington, D.C. 20004

• Books about historic preservation.
• Newsletter with membership.

LOCAL "OWNER BUILDER" CENTER
Some communities have educational organizations for the homeowner who wants to build his or her own home. They may offer the following:

• Classes and seminars on how to build, remodel and repair your home yourself.
• Bookstore.
• Advertises consulting services.
• Provides a contractor referral network.

YOUR COMMUNITY GOVERNMENT BUILDING AGENCIES
Building Department
Planning Department
Zoning Department
Usually located at your city or county government building.

• Defines community regulations about building, remodeling and adding onto a home.
• Provides information about how to build to satisfy regulations.
• May provide pamphlets or brochures about home remodeling.

Bibliography

This book presents an overview of the many steps involved in a home remodeling project. Additional books will provide design ideas, in-depth information about a specific building subject and details about how to do it yourself. There are many books on the market and I recommend that you browse through your local bookstores to find those which appeal to you. Magazines and local newspapers often feature articles about some aspects of remodeling, too. I used the following books and periodicals for infomation and inspiration for this book. They may be helpful to you, also.

Books

American Institute of Architects. *Architect's Handbook of Professional Practice.*
Washington, D.C.: The American Institute of Architects, 1973.
Three volumes about the practice of architecture; contains procedures and contract forms.

American Institute of Architects (David Haviland). *You and Your Architect.* Washington D.C.: The American Institute of Architects, 1986.
A pamphlet describing how to establish and maintain a professional relationship between an owner and an architect.

Ching, Francis D.K. and Dale E. Miller. *Home Renovation.* New York: Van Nostrand Reinhold Company, Inc., 1983.
Discusses planning and design considerations for home renovation; describes design features, materials, construction methods and details with many helpful illustrations.

City of Palo Alto. *Residential Construction Guide.* Palo Alto, California: City of Palo Alto.
This pamphlet outlines basic construction requirements.

Conran, Terence. *New House Book.* New York: Villard Books, 1985.
An update of the *House Book.* A large volume of design ideas for exterior and interior remodeling and furnishings. Numerous photographs, illustrations and descriptions.

Contractors State License Board, State of California, Department of Consumer Affairs. *Blueprint for Building Quality.* Sacramento: Contractors State License Board, 1980.
A pamphlet describing how to work with contractors.

Crane, Catherine C. *What Do You Say to a Naked Room?* New York: The Dial Press, 1979.
A practical guide about interior design for the homeowner.

Curran, June. *Drawing Home Plans.* Carmichael, California: Brooks Publishing Company, 1979.
Describes how to draw your own house plans.

Editors of Rodale's New Shelter. *Homeowner's Handbook, Working With Contractors*. Emmaus, Pennsylvania: Rodale Press, Inc., 1986.
 A pamphlet describing the alternatives of working with a contractor or being your own contractor.

Gilliatt, Mary. *The Decorating Book*. New York: Pantheon Books, 1981.
 Discusses principles of interior design, room by room design guide, samples and furnishings.

Goddard, Michael C. and Mike and Ruth Wolverton. *How to be Your Own Architect*. Blue Ridge Summit, Pennsylvania: Tab Books, Inc., 1985.
 Describes how to draw your own house plans, prepare specifications, obtain bids from contractors and get permits.

Healey, Deryck. *Living With Color*. Chicago, Illinois: Rand McNally & Company, 1982.
 Describes how to work with color for interiors and explains some history of the use of color.

Heldman, Carl. *Manage Your Own Home Renovation*. Pownal, Vermont: Storey Communications, Inc. 1987.
 Restoring or remodeling older homes: finding, buying, rebuilding and acting as your own general contractor.

Krotz, Joanna L. *Metropolitan Home Renovation Style*. New York: Villard Books, 1986.
 Case studies of renovations. Many design ideas, photographs and helpful hints.

Lester, Kent and Una Lamie. *The Complete Guide to Remodeling Your Home*. White Hall, Virginia: Betterway Publications, Inc. 1987.
 A manual for homeowners and investors; how to evaluate, select, estimate costs and be the general contractor for a home remodeling project.

McGuerty, Dave, and Kent Lester. *The Complete Guide to Contracting Your Home*. White Hall, Virginia: Betterway Publications, Inc., 1986.
 A workbook and guide for the owner who acts as general contractor for construction work on his or her home.

Ortho Books Editors. *Ortho's Home Improvement Encyclopedia*. San Francisco: Ortho Books, 1985.
 An encyclopedia of how almost everything in your house works and is put together. Useful for repairs and maintenance.

Ortho Books Editors. Series on building, remodeling and home and garden design including:
 How to Plan and Design Additions.
 How to Design and Remodel Kitchens.
 How to Design and Remodel Bathrooms.
 How to Plan and Remodel Attics and Basements.
 San Francisco: Ortho Books, 1980-.
 Ortho publishes numerous books about designing and remodeling all parts of your home and garden.

Prentice, Helen Kaplan and Blair Prentice, City of Oakland Planning Department. *Rehab Right*. Berkeley, California: Ten Speed Press, 1986.
 A manual for remodeling and rehabilitating older homes.

Roskind, Robert. *Before You Build, A Preconstruction Guide*. Berkeley, California: Ten Speed Press, 1981.
What to consider and do before you decide to build; for people who want to build their own homes (i.e. do their own construction).

Sudjic, Deyan. *The Lighting Book, A Complete Guide to Lighting Your Home*. New York: Crown Publishers, Inc., 1985.
Describes types of lighting for the home; includes many photographs.

Sunset Books and Magazine Editors. Series on building, remodeling and home and garden design including:
Add-a-Room Book.
Planning and Remodeling Bathrooms.
Planning and Remodeling Kitchens.
Remodeling Your Home.
Menlo Park, California: Lane Publishing Company, 1976-.
Sunset publishes numerous books about designing and remodeling all parts of your home and yard.

Talamo, John. *The Real Estate Dictionary*. Boston, Massachusetts: Financial Publishing Company, 1979.
A pocket dictionary of real estate and building terms.

Other books which can offer historical background and/or good reading are:

Kidder, Tracy. *House*. Boston, Massachusetts: Houghton Mifflin Company, 1985.
A novel about building a house in the eastern United States.

McAlester, Virginia and Lee. *A Field Guide to American Homes*. New York: Alfred A. Knopf, 1985.
Descriptions and identification of American building styles.

Poppeliers, John C., S. Allen Chambers, Jr. and Nancy B. Schwartz. *What Style Is It?*. Washington, D.C.: The Preservation Press, National Trust for Historic Preservation, 1983.
A pocket guide to American architectural styles.

Rybczynski, Witold. *Home, A Short History of an Idea*. New York: Viking Penguin Inc., 1986.
A discussion of the concept "home", a history of its evolution and our ideas of what makes it comfortable.

Periodicals

Baker, Kermit and Elizabeth Baatz. "Residential Construction Off to a Blazing Start," *Profesional Builder*, (July 1986), 22-23+.

Banks, William C. "Buy a House That Needs Paint," *Money*, (April 1986), 66-68+.

"Buying Furniture," *Bay Area Consumers' Checkbook*, 3, No. 3, (Fall 1986) 2-20.
An excellent consumer article about evaluating furniture and where to purchase it in the San Francisco Bay Area.

Coffett, Beth. "Drafting the Home Team," *Metropolitan Home*, (March 1986), 31-32, 36-39.

Hirst, Arlene. "Furniture Frustration: Why It Is So Hard to Get the Goods," *Metropolitan Home*, (September 1986), 46-51, 106-107.

"Home Improvements: What They Cost, What They Pay Back," *Good Housekeeping*, 204, No. 4 (April 1987), 188-191, 205.

McGrath, Ann, and Cindy Skrzycki. "Does Adding On a Room Pay Off?" *U.S. News and World Report;* cited in the *San Francisco Chronicle* (April 9, 1986), n.pag.

Miller, Jack. "Boom in Remodeling Jobs Brings Warnings," *San Francisco Sunday Examiner and Chronicle,* (July 1, 1984), N-39, N-40.

"Remodeling Jobs Don't Always Improve Value," *Popular Mechanics*; cited in the *San Francisco Sunday Examiner and Chronicle*, (April 27, 1986), R-6.

Rubenstein, Nathan. "Residential Alterations and Repairs," *Construction Review*, (September/October 1984), 5-17.

Stewart, Jon. "Beware of Risks When Buying a Fixer-Upper Home," *San Francisco Sunday Examiner and Chronicle*, (February 2, 1986), H-1, H-6.

Vila, Bob. "Home Improvements That Pay," *Real Estate Today, Home Guide*, (1986), 65-70.

Index

NOTE:
• Listings in Italics are Worksheets.
• Additional terms used in remodeling are defined in the *Glossary*.

Photographs of Remodeled Home

Date _____

Use this page to attach photographs of your home AFTER your home remodeling.

Photographs of Remodeled Home

Date _____

Use this page to attach photographs of your home AFTER your home remodeling.

Photographs of Remodeled Home

Date_____

Use this page to attach photographs of your home AFTER your home remodeling.

Notes

Notes

Notes